Praise for

With BrainWorking Recursive Therapy, Terence Watts has developed a method that can lead to significant brain change and well-being for people that suffer from anxiety, phobias, guilt, mild to moderate depression and other conditions that impact daily life functioning. This method has had a significant impact on numerous lives already and is conducted by therapists worldwide. This is the first self-help book utilising this method and you will be guided step by step by Terence towards dealing with your problems in a completely new, groundbreaking way.

Åsa Hammar, Professor and Specialist in Clinical Neuropsychology, Faculty of Psychology, University of Bergen

You, those you love and those you help are about to take a quantum leap. BWRT is brilliant. All that awaits is your best life. You will be startled by the approach's simplicity and excited to share the results with everyone you know.

Kevin Hogan, author of *The Psychology of Persuasion* and *The Science of Influence*

Here is a book whose psychological foundation about dysfunctional behaviours is solid. The problem behaviours covered include guilt, anxiety, self-worth, generalised anxiety disorder (GAD), phobias and depression, among others. Terence focuses on those problem behaviours common to humanity and makes the explanations of these dysfunctional behaviours understandable to the layperson. Indeed, much of the book's content is a readable behavioural description of those problem behaviours and they are worth far more than the cost of the book. What makes the key difference, however, are the several step-by-step patterns – the aim of which is to make dysfunctional behaviours functional.

Bobby G. Bodenhamer, author and NLP psychotherapist and trainer

Terence Watts is an outstanding hypnotherapy professional with a sterling past. Not only did he found one of the most credible hypnosis associations in the world, he is also a published author of other books that have helped the hypnotherapy profession. His latest book, on BWRT, is another valuable contribution to the evolving hypnotherapy profession. In my opinion, the writings of Terence Watts will be influencing hypnotherapy students and professionals alike for the next century and beyond. If you want new ideas, get this book!

Roy Hunter, author and hypnosis instructor

In this book Terence Watts provides a brilliantly simple way to conceptualise the complex array of neural subsystems responsible for many of our problematic reactions, decisions and actions. Furthermore, he presents a clear summary of the specific steps needed to accomplish the essence of effective therapy – i.e. the development of a clear sense of how one's future will feel once those problematic reactions, decisions and actions have been replaced and the incorporation of that imagined future into the present.

Ronald A. Havens, PhD, Professor Emeritus in Psychology,
University of Illinois Springfield

This is a totally accessible book, written with an ongoing passion and sensitivity for the needs of the reader. It is written flexibly and avoids the unnecessary use of technical language wherever possible. Terence's enthusiastic, compassionate and affirming voice comes through in his writing. The framing of the text, the helpful strategies and the extracts of the salient points of each chapter provide a unique depth to the book, which makes it a valuable resource and a must-read.

Dr Dirke A. de Villiers, educational psychologist, BWRT practitioner,
and founder of MindScienceWorx

Terence Watts created BWRT – one of the most powerful therapies, if not *the* most powerful therapy, for helping resolve emotional and psychological difficulties – and has now made it accessible to everyone in this incredibly comprehensive and detailed book. You will find an understanding of how problems can develop and how BWRT gets it sorted, which leads into the step-by-step process of dealing with a wide range of mental health issues, including self-worth, the different types of anxiety, depression, phobias, performance enhancement, boosting the immune system and more. Terence's easy style of writing makes it simple to understand the therapeutic process and to quickly start reaping the rewards of resolving uncomfortable and distressing problems.

Keith Tunstall, anxiety therapist, BWRT UK, and hypnotherapist

The BWRT method explained in the book is extremely user-friendly and highly effective. I am greatly impressed with how much this book offers to readers. It is a worthy read for anyone, including BWRT professionals!

Dr Elisa Mecco, clinical psychologist and BWRT practitioner

Terence rides the wave of cutting-edge science application in a self-help format. With clear instructions and word-for-word scripts, he makes it possible for *anyone* to tackle their issues at root level. And best of all, it can (and should) be completely customised and personalised.

Dr Feroza Arbee, specialist psychiatrist in private practice

The exercises in this book will show you just how powerful your mind is and just what you can achieve when you work in harmony with your mind and body. Enjoy discovering the different ways BWRT can work for you, along with the amazing changes you will make.

Gillian Sinclair, BWRT practitioner, trainer and supervisor

The book is a groundbreaking work from a true visionary. It is commendable that Watts has shared his pioneering work as there is no doubt that BWRT will have a far-reaching and indelible impact on mental health and well-being worldwide.

Professor Kathryn Anne Nel, PhD, Research Associate, University of Limpopo, and counselling psychologist

If you are after a self-help book that will restore you, skip all the others and buy this one. It is a gift to the world with its incredibly detailed technique on how to repair, reset and reorganise in a short period of time. Medication-free, available 24/7 and with no side-effects.

Dr Olessya Burgess, Cairns Life Therapy

Imagine suddenly discovering that there's a user manual for your life – one that sets forth in clear, easy-to-grasp terms exactly how to go about clearing up the issues that plague you and enhancing your strengths. Well, this is it! Terence Watts has provided a do-it-yourself book with step-by-step instructions on applying BWRT principles. There's even a 'maintenance guide' in the form of a daily and weekly plan. Terence has the ability to explain technical information in a way that's concise, informal and gives you the occasional chuckle too! For anyone wanting to live their best life, this book is a must-have.

Sumedha Bhise, psychotherapist

Written with great clarity and intelligence, Terence Watts' book provides readers with an understanding of human nature that is both unique and thought-provoking, and an insight into the amazing therapy that is BWRT. BrainWorking Recursive Therapy logically makes sense from both an evolutionary and neuroscientific perspective, and the self-help tools in this book are easy to follow and really do make a difference!

Sue Learoyd-Smith, PhD, trauma therapist,
BWRT practitioner and supervisor

Terence Watts is a gifted innovator whose remarkable BWRT technique is transforming lives. With this book he makes this powerful approach available so that you can overcome your biggest challenges – from self-worth to fears, phobias, anxiety and more. The book truly contains the possibility to change your life in deep and profound ways with a simplicity and depth never before possible. Terence guides you confidently through the practical exercises with clarity using his many decades of experience as a therapist. His writing is clear and accessible and you can feel his warmth and knowledge shining through every page. Each chapter reveals gems that will help you understand what's been upsetting you for years and allow you to dissolve your issue smoothly and quickly in a way that just might surprise you.

Dr Tony Fitzgerald, PhD, founder of Predicting Better

BWRT®

Reboot your life with
BrainWorking Recursive Therapy

Terence Watts

Crown House Publishing Limited
www.crownhouse.co.uk

Published by
Crown House Publishing
Crown Buildings, Bancyfelin, Carmarthen, Wales, SA33 5ND, UK
www.crownhouse.co.uk

and

Crown House Publishing Company LLC
PO Box 2223, Williston, VT 05495, USA
www.crownhousepublishing.com

First published 2022. Reprinted 2022.

Cover image © Anita Ponne – stock.adobe.com

British Library of Cataloguing-in-Publication Data
A catalogue entry for this book is available from the British Library.

Print ISBN 978-178583598-8
Mobi ISBN 978-178583611-4
ePub ISBN 978-178583612-1
ePDF ISBN 978-178583613-8

LCCN 2021950844

Printed and bound in the UK by
CPI Antony Rowe, Chippenham, Wiltshire

Dedicated to my amazing wife, the redoubtable Julie Watts, who patiently listened to all my ramblings about BWRT in the very beginning when it made hardly any sense.

Foreword

I have been a practicing clinical psychologist for 31 years at the date of writing this. During this time, I have spent ten years lecturing in the Department of Psychology, in the Faculty of Community and Health Sciences at the University of the Western Cape in Cape Town. I had also spent some time lecturing at the Department of Medically Applied Psychology at the University of Natal in Durban, South Africa. I met Terence Watts quite by accident. I was doing a clinical hypnotherapy course and in the training manual were several scripts for enhancing deep relaxation. One script immediately looked and felt different. It stood out for me from the routine, boring old scripts I had become accustomed to and was still using in my daily work. I could tell that this was written by someone who was a very different thinker. I was struck by the clarity of thought, the beauty of expression and the crisp, logical flow of ideas. It was written by a person called Terence Watts. I googled him and came to a website called Hypnosense, which I discovered, at that time, was a treasure trove of books and DVDs for anyone doing psychotherapy. I became an excellent customer and bought several of his books!

It made an immediate difference in my clinical practice, and I found that I was able to help my patients faster and more effectively using Terence's techniques and methods. Then about two years later he advertised that he was doing an online course on a new therapeutic technique called BrainWorking Recursive Therapy (BWRT®). After having used Terence's work, I had high regard for his credibility. I signed up for it in October 2013 and the course blew my mind. His concepts and ideas challenged me like nothing had ever done before, forcing me to think differently. BWRT was like nothing I had learned or taught before.

I was excited and intrigued by what I was learning. I had a thriving clinical psychology practice and ran a therapy clinic for inpatient treatment. This clinic generally admitted patients suffering from depression, severe anxiety, post-traumatic stress disorder, sexual abuse, grief, obsessive-compulsive disorder (OCD) and other mental health conditions. I was excited to try this new therapy, with the patient's permission of course, in the safe and protected environment of the clinic. I was astounded by the unexpected rapidity and effectiveness of the treatment. It was then that I realised fully that this therapy was going to revolutionise the world of psychotherapy. I then became Terence's research partner and helped to further develop BWRT into the amazing worldwide success that it has now become.

BWRT has absolutely changed the way I practice therapy as a clinical psychologist. I began to teach it to other psychologists, psychiatrists and clinical social workers in South Africa and they all had the same incredible experience with BWRT in their practices. It is now being used at university student counselling centres, some school psychological services, several departments of correctional services, prison psychological services, by several military psychologists and by the South African police psychological services.

This book has been a long time in the making, and its time has finally come. There has never been a more appropriate time for such a book to be written. We are still amid what seems to be an endless pandemic of COVID-19 where the mental health needs of ordinary people have been catapulted to centre stage. With this has come the realisation that there will never be enough experienced psychotherapists to deal with the explosion in mental health issues that have emerged because of the worldwide pandemic. This book, I believe, will go a long way to addressing that vital need. Terence has written a book about a complex therapy in a very simple way. He has made real self-help truly available to the ordinary man and woman who may not otherwise have access to specialised psychotherapeutic expertise. Of course, this book does not in any way promote itself as the answer to all mental health problems for everyone, but it does open the way for people who may not previously have considered getting help for a variety of reasons: such as fear of stigma, financial reasons, geographical location or the belief that therapy is long and complicated and exhausting. But now help is immediately available in this incredible book. Terence has made help easily accessible. There are hundreds of self-help books available all over the world, but this one is special.

It *will do* what it promises to do in simple, achievable steps that everyone can do, and the best part? In many cases almost immediate results are achievable.

In my years as a senior academic I was privileged to attend many conferences around the world and meet many of the most famous people in the field of psychology. People whose textbooks I'd read as a student, people whose textbooks I had prescribed to my undergraduate students at university, people whose work I had taught to my master's students in psychology.

In my opinion Terence Watts is right up there with the best of them, and in many ways, better. The man is, in a word, a genius. This book is going to transform the self-help industry the way that BWRT has transformed the world of psychotherapy.

Rafiq Lockhat, clinical psychologist
Cape Town, South Africa

Acknowledgements

With much gratitude to Rafiq Lockhat, who became my research partner almost as soon as I had taught the process for the first time.

Thanks also to all the early pioneers of BWRT, whose unwavering support in the face of much initial scepticism was greatly valued.

Contents

What It Is and How It Works

First, a disclaimer: BrainWorking Recursive Therapy (BWRT) was only taught for the first time in 2013 so is still, in therapy terms, very new. But from the beginning it has astounded all who have studied the training and as a result it has been eagerly adopted by thousands of clinical psychologists, psychiatrists, counsellors and other therapists worldwide, including professors of psychology. They are using it on an everyday basis, often in preference to any other therapy, to relieve suffering and, in many cases, save lives. It is also in use by some police and military because of its ability to rapidly resolve post traumatic stress disorder (PTSD).[1]

BWRT is a new process; it was initially met with scepticism, with therapists insisting there could be nothing in it that had not been taught before and that it could not possibly be as effective as was being claimed. It was first taught to a small group of professional therapists in October 2013, all of whom instantly recognised that it was something genuinely new and different and not just a rehash of one of the dozens – hundreds, probably – of other available therapies. They were impressed by the fact that BWRT is based strongly in science and evolutionary biology – and not only does it work, but, unlike the majority of other therapies, we also know exactly why it works. After that early beginning, the word spread quickly and now (in 2022) it is in worldwide use.

---

1   See https://www.bwrt.org/ and https://bwrtsa.co.za/.

And now you have a chance to use this cutting-edge therapy in the comfort of your own home.

To the uninitiated, or untrained, it can seem that BWRT is just a quick fix that fades over time because unless you find the initial sensitising event (often referred to as the ISE) the presenting problem will always return. And that is absolutely correct – as far as standard therapy models are concerned. These older therapies trawl through conscious thought, sometimes childhood, looking for anything that causes discomfort and then working on it; but those things don't actually exist in the mind, only appearing there when something triggers them into existence. BWRT, though, simply disables them at source. To give a simple analogy, if uncomfortable symptoms were like water flowing from a hose, older therapies seek to make the stream less powerful whereas BWRT simply turns off the tap.

You'll discover more about the way BWRT works and how it does so in Chapter 1. But first it's important to recognise that as good as this self-help is, it doesn't pretend to be as effective as if you had a session with a registered BWRT practitioner. There's actually a very sound reason for this. When you attend a session as a client, the practitioner does most of the work and all you have to do is relax and follow what they're saying; it's really very easy to get a super result in only one or two sessions for even quite complicated problems. Most of the time you would only have to tell them how you feel about something and how you would like to feel instead and they can get straight to work – you don't even have to tell them about anything you'd rather keep to yourself, either. But with the self-help model, you have to become both therapist and client at the same time; your brain is tasked with thinking of two things at once or switching quickly between them. Having said that, the special procedures provided in this book mean you will, more often than not, be able to do what BWRT does best: enable your brain to completely overwrite whatever problem you're experiencing with new information. You'll discover exactly how to create the perfect replacement information from your own thoughts and, because it's your own idea, your brain will happily accept it.

The sequence of therapy used in this book is identical to that which the professional therapist uses, though they employ slightly different techniques to enhance concentration and focus. Essentially, though, the routine is based around the same concepts:

- Bring the problem vividly to mind.
- Disable it within seconds (that really can happen when you know h
- Replace how it feels with how you want to feel.
- Create a high level of intensity to emphasise its importance.
- Show the brain a vivid future where the problem no longer exists.
- Create what's called a *recursive loop* to lock it all in place.
- Test and repeat if necessary.

There are several different life issues you can choose to work with, although you may, of course, decide to work on every single one of them. And it will get easier every time. You should always complete at least Chapters 1–6 before starting to work with any of the problems covered in the book, for two reasons: (1) you will gain a thorough understanding of how BWRT works; and (2) Chapters 4–6 in particular provide a solid framework upon which to base your new life. Also, at the end of Chapter 2, there's a special relaxing and stabilising routine you will need in order to finish each therapy procedure. It's called the Super Unwind and it's in two parts, each of which can be used separately.

Two ways to work

Just like the professional version of BWRT, what you're learning in this book will provide a completely personalised therapy that is customised specifically to the way your brain and mind works. In each procedure, there's a full technical description of the 'events' techniques that are employed. One way to work is to just read through them carefully, giving your full attention to each step, and where it says something like 'Repeat steps 3–6 five more times' then do so with complete concentration. But it's inestimably better to do a little more to create a self-help therapy most closely resembling that of a professional environment, which will give you the best mental healthcare possible with self-help. This simply involves recording the procedure for whatever you want to sort out, exactly as it's written down in the *text to record* scripts in the book. You only need to do this once for any problem you want to fix. These are no ordinary therapy scripts, for two reasons:

1. BWRT is no ordinary therapy and lends itself to a specific structure. The structure and design are shown in more detail in the *reading* version before you get to the written script material. You don't have

to read the technical structure if you don't want to – you can just go directly to the *text to record* section and that will work perfectly.

2. The scripts are written in *speaking* style and personalised to fit your psyche and processes of thought exactly, making them ultra-effective. Always keep the volume normal, even where you're using emphasis, because loudness isn't necessary and doesn't actually work very well for BWRT.

Read the script into your mobile phone or digital recorder so that you can later sit back and follow along – ideally with your eyes closed to enhance concentration and imagination, just as you would within a professional setting. Everything is written up with clear instructions for you to follow, showing where you need emphasis and even explaining how to create the right atmosphere. You can change the wording a little if you need to make it sound more like the sort thing you might usually say (though it's not really necessary) – but if you decide to do that, be quite certain not to change the meaning, since the texts are carefully worded.

Quite often you'll be reading a series of statements five or six times, but it doesn't have to be word perfect, nor do you have to use a therapy-style voice – whatever your voice is like will be just fine (mistakes, stumbles, stutters and coughs included). Now, this might sound a bit strange since you'd expect it was important that everything was crystal clear, but it's not the words that do the job here – it's the concept behind them. You will have already primed a special part of the brain (discussed later in Chapter 1) with the concept while you were creating the procedure and the repetition of the words is just to reinforce the importance of it. When your alarm clock goes off, you don't think 'I'll just lie here for a few more minutes' or 'I must get up straight away today', even though you know that's what you're going to do. You're acting on the concept and that's exactly what will be happening with BWRT. It's another of the differences between this and other therapies, almost all of which rely on conscious understanding of what is being said. This is because they work through the higher part of the brain, while BWRT goes straight to the part that other therapies don't always reach.

Much more than you expect

Because BWRT is so efficient, it can often do in one chapter what might take an entire book with the more standard forms of therapy – hence there are far more opportunities within these pages to improve your life than you might expect. In the beginning, you'll discover the *how* and *why* and after an experiential exercise to whet your appetite you'll find out about the *what*, which includes:

- Defusing the subconscious stress attached to secrets in the darkest corners of your mind (everybody has an embarrassing secret; you can still keep the secret but lose the embarrassment).
- Super-tuning your immune system to keep your body as healthy as it can be so you can enjoy life to the full.
- Preparing to get the very best out of the major changes you're going to make.
- Boosting your self-worth; what you've been taught about yourself shapes what you think about yourself – but a lot of it is fake news.
- Dealing with the aftermath of problems created during your early years and preparing for major change.
- Understanding anxiety in all its different forms, why we have it and why we just don't need it most of the time.
- Banishing generalised anxiety disorder (GAD) for good – this psychologically crippling disorder seems to find its way into everything.
- Getting a grip of free-floating anxiety and letting go of those anxious moments that seem to keep on popping up for no reason you can think of.
- Dealing with the simple phobia, even when it seems far from simple, and getting rid of it for good.
- The complex phobia conundrum – it might not even be a true phobia but BWRT can still fix it.
- Performance enhancement – harnessing the resources you thought you had but weren't sure how to find.
- Releasing mild to moderate depression via a two-step process that can amaze you with its ability to lift you out of the doldrums.
- Core identity issues covered in two chapters that show you how to let go of the you you're fed up with and adopt the perfect persona.
- Planning for the ideal future, now that light has been shone into the darkest corners of your mind and you can look where you're going.
- The daily maintenance plan; working with your inherited personality to make life even easier and how to find professional help if you need it.

There's a bit of ground to cover before you get to the process proper though, and a few exciting things to make sense of – so turn the page to Chapter 1 and let's get started.[2]

2 *For professional therapists*
What you are reading in this book is based on the same process that the professional BWRT practitioner uses and achieves excellent results. But you will appreciate that it's been formulated specifically to get the best result within the boundaries of self-perception and the familiarity of one's own thought processes, voice patterns and cadences. For that reason it is highly recommended that you do not seek to use the material in this book as a therapist with a client, since the results are unpredictable. The professional routines work differently using material designed to entrain the processes of the deepest part of the client's psychology with an awareness of delivery from an authority source.

Chapter 1

Just Who Makes Up Your Mind?

If you've skipped the introduction, please go back and read it – otherwise some of what you find here and later will make no sense at all!

Ever knocked something off a shelf with one hand and caught it with the other without thinking? Even if you weren't quite quick enough, that other hand probably still gave it a shot before you knew it. You don't think about it and don't even know you're going to do it – and although it might not make much sense at this stage, you've just read about the key to almost every psychological problem you will ever experience; a special part of your brain starts to do stuff before you know it.

Now, you might think we're talking here about that rather mysterious entity, the subconscious. Well, there's a very odd truth about the subconscious – it doesn't actually exist, so you can't send your thoughts to the part of you that so many self-help books and various therapies need you to work with. You can think of your nose or your left big toe (and probably just did) but as soon as you try to think about the subconscious, you end up with either a dark mysterious place full of secrets that you don't even know about or a shadowy version of you that's not too keen on letting you know what's going on there – and even less keen on making permanent change.

The term *subconscious* was coined in 1889 by the French psychologist Pierre Janet[1] – probably to refer to the fact that there is definitely something going on in the psyche, beneath the level of conscious thought. Over the last 130-odd years it has become almost a buzz word for anything to do with uncomfortable or unwanted behaviour or thoughts because there was nothing better to call it. It's used as a matter of course by psychiatrists, psychologists and just about anybody interested in or working with the human mind. Nonetheless, it's really nothing more than an idea – a concept – and certainly not a physical part of the body that we can send our thoughts to or try to manipulate; and manipulation is definitely needed if you want to make huge and fast changes to the way you function in the world.

So, if it's not the subconscious that does all that under-the-counter stuff, what is it? Well, it's almost certainly a truly physical part of the body – the lizard brain, sometimes referred to as the reptilian complex (which this book will do from now on). This ancient part of the brain came into being, as far as anyone knows, over 600 million years ago, in some of the earliest animals on Earth. It was actually the only brain they had and it had to do absolutely everything: looking after the vital processes like circulation, respiration, digestion, body repairs and everything else. Back then, of course, *everything else* was pretty much just feeding and breeding – and staying alive in order to do more of the other two.

You might now be wondering what on earth this has to do with catching a vase you've just knocked off a shelf. Well, a lot more than you might think. You see, those early animals were creatures of instinct and nothing more. They lived or died by the accuracy of those instincts – it was nothing to do with weighing up a situation and assessing the best response. There wasn't time for any of that and survival depended purely on an instinctive response to a threat: run like the devil or fight like a demon; try to escape the enemy or try to kill it before it kills you. That bit of the brain is a lot older than conscious thought and far, far quicker. It was the first responder to life and all there was for well over 550 million years, during the later part of which evolution had seen to it that some animals had developed a more sophisticated process capable of a wider range of emotional responses. And then, only around 3 million years ago, the biggest part of the brain – the cerebral cortex – appeared, purportedly in the early humans. But that

---

1   K. Bühler and G. Heim, Pierre Janets Konzeption des Unterbewussten [Pierre Janet's Conception of the Subconscious]. *WÜrzburger medizinhistorische Mitteilungen* 27 (2008): 24–62. Available at: https://pubmed.ncbi.nlm.nih.gov/19230366/.

reptilian complex still remains the first responder – it can't not, because evolution just doesn't dump anything that works, especially when it works as well as that early brain.

So, it's still there in all of us, checking our surroundings for threat 24/7 just as it always has done. But it does something else, too. It learns how we respond to repeated actions and creates an instinctive response that it will automatically trigger when it recognises the relevant pattern of events or circumstances. That response is activated immediately, just as it would have been with those early animals millions of years ago. But the brain doesn't work anywhere near as fast as you might imagine and we don't become aware of what's going on until about half a second later, by which time it's already happening and we've saved that vase from smashing to bits. Later, we refer to that half-second as the cognitive gap and it's there that we make changes.

Of course, if that bit of the brain has triggered anxiety (or any other unwanted response) for some reason, it will already be happening by the time we become aware of it – which is exactly why it can be so difficult to get control of. And as to why it would do that, it's because it recognised something that used to be a threat; it might not be so now, but nobody told the reptilian complex that. There are many other responses but they all come down to the same thing: that reptilian complex has spotted a pattern to which it has a response that must be activated because it's there.

What this means is that you don't have free will in the way you usually think of it. Just about everything in your conscious mind has been processed and acted upon before you're aware of it by that reptilian complex.

You don't have free will, but you do have *free won't*. What this means is that you can sometimes decide not to act on an instinctive reaction (so you decide not to eat that scrumptious-looking cream cake) but you can't stop the urge from occurring in the first place. The reptilian complex has learned that you love cream cakes and so the urge to eat it pops up immediately – and it might be swiftly followed by a determination not to because the reptilian complex has also learned that you don't want to respond to that first urge. And in case you're wondering, the first urge has to occur so that the second one, of determination, can arise because it has linked them together.

You're probably beginning to understand why making changes to what used to be called the subconscious is so difficult. But BWRT makes it a lot easier, as you'll see later.

Just be yourself

You might have been given the advice many times to *just be yourself* or, more recently, have experienced some well-meaning individual saying you just have to be *authentic* and the world will be yours. Well, there's a big problem there, in that those who tell you those things are themselves not being themselves or authentic. It's just a soundbite. It somehow sounds and feels right but laws, social requirements and moral codes make it impossible. If you were to be authentic you would follow your instincts and urges and needs as they arose (we all have them) and ignore those social, legal and moral restrictions, no matter where you were – and you can probably work out what sort of outrage that would cause from time to time.

It is a fact that even when they would not be out of bounds, your instincts might not necessarily be good instincts. The reptilian complex just learns behaviour patterns that are often repeated, and in that part of your brain the notion of *good* and *bad* or *better* and *best* just doesn't exist. It's just data with no emotion or value judgement of any sort. That part of the brain doesn't think or reason; it just recognises a pattern and responds with what it did before. That's all. After all, if what it did led to survival, which it clearly did because you're still here, then just do the same again to survive some more and never mind the consequences. Here are some instincts that do little to improve the lives of those who have them (we're ignoring where they might have come from here):

- Men with beards are dangerous (pogonophobia).
- Spiders are massively frightening (arachnophobia).
- I'm inferior to most people.
- Everybody thinks I'm odd or weird.
- I'm jinxed – everything goes wrong.
- I am better than everyone else.
- I can do what I like – nobody should tell me what to do.

So, if your reptilian complex has learned that social situations are the source of excruciating embarrassment, for example, then it will create anxiety every time you even think about dinner parties (or anything similar) so that you develop social phobia. On the other hand, if it has learned that you can't function very well on your own, you might develop separation anxiety and become a rather clingy individual. The reptilian complex doesn't question anything – if it encounters something new, it will store it along with any reaction. If you see a spider when you're very small, you might just be curious – and that's the response that will be filed. But if, later, you see a spider and an adult runs from it screaming blue murder, the caveat *life threatening* will be added to the stimulus *spider*, completely overriding *curious* on the grounds that it's a threat to survival.

Just about everything you know is like that, based on some experience or another not necessarily personal; you know crocodiles are dangerous, and would probably panic if you found yourself in the water with one, but the only experience of that situation is almost certainly just what you've been told. You can imagine what it would be like to be so rich you could have everything you want but only because you've been told about it, perhaps in a film. Most of what you know therefore is based on what somebody else has told you of their own experience. The reptilian complex cares not one jot about that and the more times you hear/see it, the stronger the belief is that it must be so. This is the basis upon which you learn every single thing in life. It's why, if you come up against something you just don't recognise, you stop for a moment while you try to find out more about it. Maybe only for a fraction of a second, but you still stop. And that stop is vitally important to BWRT, as you will shortly see. Before we get to that though, there's something else to get your head around – and it might be something of a surprise.

A simple bit of kit

Everybody knows the brain is the most complex thing in the entire universe, right? Physically, that's definitely the case. It has around 86 billion neurons, over 80 per cent of which are in that reptilian complex. That means that around 69 billion neurons are making the decision about what the other 17 billion should be doing, and only some of those 17 billion (nobody knows how many for sure) are involved in conscious awareness. But those 69 billion are doing only one of three things with every impulse that comes in from the outside world:

- It's safe: continue.
- It's unsafe: take avoiding action.
- Unknown: wait to find out more.

third one, the 'Unknown: wait to find out more' is the freeze response
ch tends to happen in any emergency when we just don't know what to
uc. It's probable that there is no stored response that fits, hence the brain
can do nothing until there's more information, and all it can do is wait. So,
we have fight, flight or freeze, and that is all that part of the brain does –
routing the response, when there is one, to a part of the far more
complicated cerebral cortex for action. It is doing that very same thing in
response to every split second of every experience we have, just as it did
for those most ancient ancestors of ours 600-plus million years ago. And it
is the very same process that we use in BWRT to make rapid change.

What BWRT does

BWRT is probably the only psychological therapy model that is designed to
work directly in that cognitive gap between the reptilian complex responding to a trigger and you becoming aware of what's happening. It's not
actually the original response itself that you feel but the result of the
response. Assuming for a moment that an anxiety trigger event occurs, the
unsafe pattern is recognised by the reptilian complex which then sends a
message to a much later (evolutionarily speaking) part of the brain, the
amygdala, to generate feelings of anxiety in an attempt to get you to take
some sort of action to keep you safe. And then another process takes place
that reinforces it: you act on the feeling in some way that confirms to the
reptilian complex it's doing the right thing, so it does it some more. And
now a self-cycling feedback loop has been created. Because of this, the
stronger or more frequent the message and the stronger the feedback, the
more profound the anxiety response becomes; all the way up to terror,
when there is a perception that life itself is threatened. That's all well and
good when the threat is real, but not so good when it's not – as in the case
of a phobia of spiders, for instance. Or crane flies. Or maybe vomiting
(that's called emetophobia and is much more common than some people
realise). As you read earlier, that part of the brain doesn't rationalise things
or try to work anything out. It doesn't think – it just instantly responds.
Effectively, a button was pushed and so the bell rang.

It might seem to you that the half-second cognitive gap is a very small
window in which to work – and of course, you are absolutely right. So, we
use a simple method to create a bit more time in which to create the
needed change and the safe response to activate it – therefore, we use
totally natural brainwork to fix the problem and what you will learn here

can easily make amazing changes to a great many uncomfortable proce
and situations.

There's one other thing to be aware of before continuing: although BWRT is
a very fast therapy, this doesn't mean it's just a quick fix that wears off – far
from it. It doesn't wear off because it doesn't add anything new into your
brain to wear off, using only the thought processes and mental abilities you
used to acquire the problem in the first place. It is fair to say, though, that
as with all forms of self-help you might need to reinforce the results by
repetition sometimes – but the procedures are very logical and once they
have been used once, they are easy to repeat. However, this is another
situation in which BWRT is different; unlike other therapies, after only two
or three repeats you'll usually have a permanent fix.

Experiential Exercise: Stop the Clock

We're not going to do anything very spectacular for this first exercise – just
something that will whet your appetite for more and build some confidence that the process will work for you. Of course, if you're very lucky it
might result in completely resolving your problem (such as anxiety or
uncertainty), since it's a kind of blanket technique that is not aimed at any
situation in particular, so you can choose any problem you want to work on.
Choose something fairly simple for this one, though – something that
makes you uncomfortable, but doesn't have you running around screaming
your head off.

Just follow the steps – it works best if you can learn it and then do it with
your eyes closed (you probably won't need to record this one):

1. Imagine how you might look from the outside if the problem had
    simply gone away, and make it as vivid in your thoughts as you can.
    Don't worry if it seems daft or unlikely, or what anybody else might
    think or say if they knew – just imagine it anyway in the privacy of
    your mind and store that image of the different self anywhere in
    your thoughts. This step is the hardest part of the exercise.

2. Now think of a clock with an hour hand, a minute hand and a hand
    that shows the seconds so that you can see the clock is working.
    Make that vivid in your mind, too. (You don't have to think of both
    this image and the first one at the same time.)

3. Next, think of a time when you were experiencing the problem and
    try to find the uncomfortable feeling. It doesn't matter if you can't

find it; just trying to find it will send the right message back to the reptilian complex. Imagine how you might look from the outside at the time and make that vivid too.

4. As soon as you can find the feeling, or try your hardest to find the feeling, just imagine you can stop time somehow so that image is now locked tight in the past and you can see that the clock has stopped (or stop it in your mind if it hasn't already). In fact, everything has stopped – except you. You can just walk out of that locked scene and adopt the different self you created in step 1.
5. Now zoom right in to feel as if you actually become that different self so that it's as if you're on the inside looking out on the world, and notice how good that feels as you realise the clock has started again.
6. Repeat steps 3–5 at least three times and notice how it gets easier each time. Stop when you're happy with how you feel, or after six repeats (which is about the maximum useful number).

That exercise is an excellent first aid for all sorts of things, though it's very far from the full BWRT experience. Having said that, it produces a permanent result for some people (while others need to repeat it from time to time) and you can use it as often as you want or need to.

So here we are at the end of Chapter 1 and you're hopefully eager to discover more.

Chapter 2

It *Is* What You Think

You've now discovered that you're not actually doomed – you can make changes in your life. That little exercise at the end of the last chapter won't help you win the lottery, or turn you into a superbeing, but it will have already started the processes of change. Though you didn't know it at the time, your efforts at locking the image in the past meant that you communicated with the very part of the brain that you need to access. And that's still the case, even if you feel you didn't manage it too well – you still communicated and, as you practise the other exercises in this book, you will inevitably get better at it.

In this chapter, we're going to have a look at the mental wrestling match that is life, what your brain has to do to come out on top most of the time and the price we all have to pay for the privilege. Because there is a price, usually in one of the forms of anxiety (although it's sometimes known by its more fashionable name: stress). In truth, stress and anxiety are not really the same thing, which is discussed in a later chapter, but they will both respond well to the techniques in this book. Much of the time, you're not aware of the tug of war that's going on in your psyche – mainly because almost all of it goes on in the background of your mind and when you do notice a bit of it at any time, things like moral codes and social niceties make themselves felt (and strongly). An example might help – it's quite brief and easy to understand:

Lee meets Kim and instantly believes this is the sexiest and most wonderful person in the entire world and that they are destined to be together. It quickly becomes obvious that Kim feels the same – but is married to Lee's single parent.

Now, there is no genuine reason why Lee and Kim could not just go off together and be a couple enjoying a fulfilling sex life for as long as they want. There would be nothing illegal about it. But it is immediately evident that, were they to do so, there would be all manner of problems and recrimination including criticism, accusations of some sort of perversion, bullying or even worse – and never mind what might happen on social media. But sexual attraction is one of the most powerful and fundamental urges that has ever existed – after all, it is the very source of existence – and even with the possible problems that might arise, people like Lee and Kim do still go ahead and follow their urges. Whichever way the battle between morals, social mores and biology ends, the outcome will be the same: the creation of stress. That's because our modern world, with its man-made laws and morals, forces a complicated and uncomfortable dance between the urges of instinct and the understanding of the possible outcome – instinctive urges have been around a lot longer than morals. And when you're not able to discharge an instinctive urge for whatever reason, the result will usually be anxiety in one of its many forms.

What follows are some other situations that people sometimes find themselves in and it's quite possible that you will have personal experience of one or more of them:

- Do you just grab that item you want and run, hoping you don't get caught?
- Do you respond to rage and risk legal retribution?
- Do you give in to desire and risk losing a life partner?
- Do you win by cheating and risk exposure and ridicule?
- Do you let somebody else take the blame and tolerate the guilt?

As uncomfortable as it might feel right now, we have all – every one of us – inherited totally self-interested instincts for the most part. Our ancient hominin ancestors of 2.5 million years ago would not have survived had they not been self-focused fighters for survival. For them, it was: 'Grab what you want or need before the others do'; 'Get the best out of any situation by any means possible' [the concept of cheating didn't exist in those days]; 'Destroy anybody and anything that might be a threat'; 'Do it to them before they do it to you'; 'If rage makes you whack somebody over the head with a lump of rock, or maybe stick something horribly sharp into some important part of them, so what?'; 'Couple with somebody if you feel like it – it's nobody's business but yours.' You might want to argue that we really can't behave like that these days and you'd be right, of course. But it is a fact that you cannot control what you feel, only what you do with what you feel.

Although there are a few people who still do behave like those ancients, there are many millions more who experience the urges but immediately reject or suppress them. That's the way the civilised world works with its legal systems and moral codes – though they vary widely across the globe, too. But the important thing is that when any urge from the reptilian complex is not acted upon, it generates stress because millions of years ago it might have been vital for survival. Just because we know that we cannot act upon the urge doesn't mean we don't want to and, because we know it's wrong, the anxiety is amplified. It's possible that some people might have been able to somehow reprogram that part of their brain so that the urges never appear, but they're not likely to be reading this book (they are likely, however, to be heavily repressed individuals who find little or no joy in life, but that's another story). So, we're not going to make any attempt to alter your thoughts about the fundamentals of life and living but to reorganise the processes of that reptilian complex so that any conflicts no longer cause stress. Along the way, we'll be removing discomfort from all sorts of dark corners in the invisible part of your psyche. And it's all going to be a whole lot easier than you might think.

The ever-changing brainscape

It's easy to imagine that those 86 billion neurons in your brain are somehow like very fine wires, fixed in their proper place and carrying bio-electric pulses to wherever they're needed so that we can go effortlessly about our daily business. Well, perhaps you already realise that it's not quite that simple but it's odds-on that you're not fully aware of the spectacular process that is actually happening. When the reptilian complex sends its *stop*, *go* or *wait a minute* message, a massive amount of activity takes place like lightning. Faster, perhaps. Literally trillions of connections are being made and unmade far faster than it's remotely possible to think about them; every neuron has at least a thousand inputs and the same number of outputs to make connections to other neurons – not just to one but to several. Hundreds. Thousands, even. All at once and in an ever-changing and dynamic kaleidoscope of connections and breaks and reconnections. And as advanced as brain science has become, nobody is fully aware of what decides which connections are made or unmade and when – only that they are controlled by chemicals called neurotransmitters. The important things to be aware of are: (1) this is happening right at this very moment in your brain as you read this; (2) there is less activity in some parts of the brain while you sleep; and (3) the process started a little while before you were born and will not stop until death.

So, the wiring of the brain is ever changing and adjusting to the world as we know it – it's designed by evolution and biology to work like that, responding and reacting to the constant stream of information that it receives. And if you've learned something you didn't already know before you started reading this book, that pattern of connections is stored for future employment if necessary. And now to the point:

What this all means is that nobody is stuck the way they are, because the brain is constantly changing – and how it changes is all controlled by your thoughts, so with the right thoughts (and a bit of practice and guidance) we can begin to change it to the way you want it to be.

What were you thinking?

You might never have realised, but you are not initially in charge of what you think. You can choose what to think about but the actual words of those thoughts just appear in your brain. It's the same as not being able to choose your feelings – but just as you can control what you do with what you feel, so you can control what you do with what you think. It's a bit more complicated than that, though, because what you think depends to a large extent on what you've already thought – about everything. So, the key to

beneficial change is to steer that continuum of thought towards where you want it to go.

It starts somewhere between the reptilian complex and the conscious part of the brain, though nobody as yet has been able to ascertain exactly how and where. What we do know, though, is that it is a journey of up to 50 metres of neurological pathways in your brain, during which there is much processing and testing going on. If we can make just one change of contact between two neurons on that journey, it can result in a whole different idea appearing in consciousness. Let's suppose you've had a bit of a rocky time in romantic relationships; with a new partner you begin to fear, and there-fore look for, signs that it's starting to go wrong because it always has before. And that's exactly what you'll find because the brain tends to find what it's looking for, or even create it, and ignore everything else. But this is where BWRT can work its magic. It can make a radical change to that experience-based thinking so that you automatically know that this new relationship is not connected with the past – then you can look for what you want instead of what you fear.

You've already experimented with changing your usual train of thoughts with the little Stop the Clock exercise at the end of Chapter 1 – and if you only got the tiniest change, which lasted no more than a few minutes, you still changed the normal progression of your thoughts. And if it didn't actually work for you at all, there are only three likely possibilities; so we'll have a look at those and attempt to solve the problem:

1. You didn't make the images vivid enough or you didn't focus strongly enough. It does need a bit of concentration and focus so give it another try, with a bit more determination to get the best out of it – it really does work.

2. You didn't believe it could work for you. That's a perfect example of following the *same old same old* thought patterns; you looked to see if everything was the same afterwards instead of what had changed. Try the exercise again and expect it to produce only the tiniest change to the original feeling, which you should search for until you find it. That will be the first step to conditioning the brain to look for what you want – the first step to reconditioning that reptilian complex of yours.

3. You wanted to prove it doesn't work. This is quite a common situation and there's always a reason for it, though it can be difficult to sort out. The biggest problem is that it will stop you from getting the best results from the rest of this book – and there's no criticism here because, as you've already read, you don't decide what you think or how you feel. It's one of the situations where a professional BWRT practitioner would be able to provide help.

Now, you might have already recognised another interesting situation about all this: what you think governs who you think you are. If you're one of the lucky ones who likes yourself overall, all well and good. But if (like many) you're not too keen, it's useful to understand that whoever you think you are, that's not the version of you that others see because they're not privy to those dark corners in your mind where the messy stuff is. Just as you're not privy to theirs – and they do have them, as we all do. Now the good news: later in this book all that messy stuff in the dark corners will get a makeover and then they'll feel nowhere near as uncomfortable as they do now.

What you get is what you think

In order to illustrate as clearly as possible why that thought continuum is so important, we're going to consider two extremes now. Most people won't fit into either extreme – but equally, most people will be closer to one than the other. This applies to the whole of life, though there are very few people who are just as successful in their career as they are in relationships as they are in their chosen hobbies, etc. Their life will be variable. But learn how to condition that thought continuum, as applied to any pursuit, and you will be on your way to becoming the superbeing mentioned at the beginning of this chapter. Whether it's excelling in your career, relationships, your hobby – be that flying model aeroplanes, photography, playing football, guitar, or anything else – sorting out that thought continuum is the way to improve your lot. There's nothing new about the idea, of course. Just about every self-help book or therapy process will tell you the same thing. But they're talking about what you consciously think and, while it's easy enough to change that, it's the devil's own job to keep that change because that reptilian complex is still doing its thing and trying to avoid threat by protecting you from change. As far as it is concerned, change means the unknown and the unknown means danger, so it attempts to maintain that continuum as it has always been to date. And it usually succeeds.

So, the only way to build change that has the highest possible chance of becoming permanent is to ensure it's made at root level, i.e. in that earliest part of the brain that is the root of all thoughts and behaviour. And that's what BWRT does. It's important to remember here that it's not possible to replicate the way that a professional BWRT practitioner would work in their office; they all have many hundreds of hours of experience in the world of therapy, and an abundance of skills and specialised professional techniques at their disposal. That said, the *BWRT lite* version that you're learning to use here can make important and permanent changes far more easily than just about any other method. As to how you're going to do that, that's something for another chapter.

Super Unwind

One of the things you can do that is very nearly as good as a professional will manage is the exercise to finish this chapter of the book. It's a specific form of deep relaxation, designed as a *gain perspective and unwind* technique; it works at the very deepest part of the mind where the essence of self is centred and, as such, produces a wonderful sense of well-being. This will improve every time you practise it and if you do it on a daily basis (only a suggestion and not essential for the work of this book) you will enhance your ability to just unwind when you need to.

The reason this technique is so powerful is that you will direct your thoughts to the specific place in your body where the essence of self resides. You don't need to concentrate on staying in the moment or focusing totally on your breathing or anything of that sort; all you need to do is understand an idea, after which you'll be able to use the technique whenever you wish. It's in two parts, the first of which is astonishingly easy – for many people it feels like a form of self-hypnosis, though it's not really that. It is, though, a totally-focusing-on-*self* process which, once learned, can be done in just a few seconds. So, practise Part One until you can do it easily and immediately, which might very well be after only a couple of attempts. Here we go:

Super Unwind – Part One

The part of your body you need to focus on is the reptilian complex, which is at the base of the brain and at the top of the spine. This is where the real essence of you lives – the you that you were born to be before life messed anything up. Just let your thoughts drift around that part of you for a few moments, understanding that you are in touch with the part of you that you've inherited from your ancient ancestors of hundreds of millions of years ago.

Learn the section in italics before you do it – it doesn't have to be word-perfect, since it's the concept that's important. When you're ready, close your eyes and:

Imagine yourself – the inner you – at the very top of your head, in the bright white light of consciousness where the connections with the world are. Then, again when you're ready, imagine that inner you can float downwards through the layers of the brain, just drifting down into that brainstem and away from the outside world. You might see some sort of imagery, or it might just seem dark,

...t either way it's not important and it's different for everybody. Wait there for a few minutes or maybe just for a few seconds. There's no need to try to do anything other than notice what it feels like, since that will help you to get to this important place in your psyche very easily in the future. It's an important place because nobody else has ever been there or ever will be there, so it's pristine and carries the essence of you – the real you that nature intended. When you're ready, drift back up again through the layers of the brain, up to the top where you can once again feel contact with the outside world and open your eyes when you feel ready.

There's often a slightly strange feeling of having been somewhere else when you open your eyes; if you felt that, it means that you got the best possible result from the exercise – well done! If you didn't the first time then you might very well do so on the second or third occasion, but don't worry if not because everybody is different.

Now, practise the exercise a few times until you feel you can pretty much just drift gently into that reptilian complex whenever you choose, and when you can do that you're ready for Part Two.

Super Unwind – Part Two

This part of the exercise is what you will do while you're in that deepest part of the psyche – and because you are going to learn a concept, rather than a set of instructions or a script, it will be different each time and will perfectly match what you need in order to get the best out of it.

The concept is simple but awe-inspiring: we are all comprised of the same material that makes up the entire universe; you are literally created out of stardust – the material from which all planets and stars are formed. Every atom and molecule in your body, many billions – maybe trillions – of years ago, was once part of the vast cosmos that surrounds us in which, after countless aeons, our Sun eventually formed. Then, much later, all the planets around it – including Earth. And after many more billions of years you came into existence: a fantastic result of the creation of life and evolution; a compilation of atoms and molecules that is a perfect reflection of the universe itself.

Your internal self – the part of you that only you truly know – works in exactly the same way as that unfathomable universe. Your thoughts and reactions are created by those billions of neurons and trillions of connections somehow appearing as ideas and images in your mind, even as you're reading this. And those images – those thoughts, ideas and reactions – will be unique, based irrevocably on all that you've ever experienced.

So, the complete Super Unwind exercise is the gentle descent into the reptilian complex, followed by a period of reflecting for as long as you wish on the magnificence and endlessness of the universe – a universe of which you have always been, and will always be, a part. You can set a timer or you can rely on your brain automatically returning to normal life – some people do fall asleep (especially if suffering from sleep deprivation), so setting a timer is probably a good idea.

Now it's time to start learning how to get those thoughts and ideas into the best possible order.

Chapter 3

How BWRT Gets It Sorted

In this chapter, you're going to learn the basic procedure – in professional circles it would usually be called a protocol – that you will be using, in one form or another, to work with whatever problem you want to solve. The actual steps of the procedure will vary according to whatever is being worked on but the underlying process is always the same.

What you're learning here is a consumer version of BWRT for home use which is based on the exact same principles and techniques as the professional one, but uses a slightly different method to access that reptilian complex. It still uses the natural fight, flight and freeze processes, too – the last of which allows us to access the other two and make changes. It might well be the case that you can't actually see how that could fix your particular problem, but don't worry too much about that at this stage since all will become clear later on. It is a fact that all psychological problems come down to anxiety in one of its forms and anxiety is often referred to as 'fear spread thin' by many therapists (often attributed to C. G. Jung). Whether it's a fight or flight reaction doesn't matter – it's still anxiety and BWRT still deals with it. As long as you understand each stage as you go, you'll be able to put it all into practice perfectly when you get to the last page of this chapter.

A professional measurement

There is one thing you can do that is identical to the way that a professional BWRT practitioner works, and that is an evaluation process that allows you to measure what improvement you have made to any problem. It's called the perceived arousal level (PAL) and refers to how uncomfortable a problem feels on a scale of 1 to 10, where 10 is very high. You check the score before the work and again afterwards (though there is quite a bit to do between the two) to see how much it has improved. There's more about that later, though you can have a practice if you feel like it by scoring one of the problems you want to work with. If it's too uncomfortable, imagine you're looking at it from the outside (technically that's called dissociated and it's one of the tricks professionals use to take the heat out of something); ideally, the score will be 8 or higher for the best results. You'll almost always get that PAL on whatever you choose to work with. For practice, though, you're going to work with something relatively mild to let you get used to the process. So now think of something that is a bit uncomfortable – nothing major, just something that leaves you feeling slightly uneasy, and get the PAL. If it's a score of 4 or 5, that'll be perfect. We'll be coming back to that later in this chapter.

New You

This stage is all about creating new neural threads in the reptilian complex to carry a different message about whatever you're working with to the part of the brain that feels stuff. To decide what that message is to be, you will need to choose any two of the following psychological responses – at least one of which must come from set 1 – which you will combine to make the best new response you can think of:

Set 1	Set 2
enthusiastic	cautious
relaxed	careful
energised	aware
relieved	watchful
happy	accepting
calm	sensible
confident	tolerant
at ease	

It's best to select a response from those listed, rather than decide to add something else, since those in both lists have been carefully chosen and are known to be safe. There are three different types of problem you might work with:

1. Anything where there is no genuine reason for the f
    though you know this it still makes you feel anxious,
    or frightened – maybe even terrified. Fear of spiders .
    are examples of this group.

2. This is much broader and includes everything where th.
    reason to be frightened, even though it might be only t   .ying
    and driving are well-known issues that come into this group.

3. Anything that involves other people, even though there's no reason
    for the fear. It includes social phobia, eating in restaurants, talking on
    the telephone, etc.

Sometimes the second type of problem might also involve people, as in the
third type, and you'll find out more about that in later chapters. For now, it's
sufficient to understand that if your problem is clearly in (1) then you must
choose both your two new response words from set 1. *Calm* and *at ease*,
perhaps. Or maybe *relaxed* and *happy*. If it's in either (2) or (3) you would
choose one response word from set 1 and the other from Set 2; so you
might decide on *calm* but *cautious* for instance, or *relaxed* but *watchful*. It
doesn't matter at all if you can't get anywhere near believing you could be
calm and at ease with a massive spider running around the room – we
haven't done the work yet.

Choose your two words (joined with *and* or *but* to make sense) to suit the
problem you've decided to work with – we'll say *relaxed* and *calm* for this
example – and think of another situation where you actually are relaxed
and calm. It's best if this image is not immediately connected with the
problem you've chosen to work with. Notice where you feel those
responses in your body – it might be your chest, torso, shoulders or arms
but wherever it is, it's right for you. This will be the New You image you will
use for the full procedure.

Ideal Future

It's important to give your reptilian complex a view into the future so it
accepts that the changes you will be making can become instantly
accepted, and this is easier than you might at first believe. Do be sure to be
totally realistic throughout, though – you can't become a true superbeing,
no matter how much work you do. Realism is key.

First of all, imagine somebody experiencing the exact problem you've chosen to work with and looking as if they feel like that New You you've just

..d, as you look in from the outside and imagine stopping time in the ..ame way you did in the Stop the Clock exercise. Now the scene becomes stationary and you can swap yourself over with that person. Stay there for just a few seconds, then come back out of it and notice the scene no longer has the other person in it, but is waiting for you to return later on. You'll frequently create the Ideal Future image for whatever you work on (though not every single time) and we'll be covering it again in the relevant parts of the book – for the moment you're just learning the procedure with that not-too-bad memory, just to get the idea.

Stop and Stare

It's an important fact that by the time you know what you're thinking of, it's old news as far as the reptilian complex is concerned. It might just as well have happened yesterday or last year. It's a done deal and cannot be changed; so if we tried to work with that, we would be using one of the older styles of therapy. The problem there is that it's slow, prone to error and the changes don't always take root straight away, needing more sessions to cement them in place. And that creates its own problem: it's very well known that the greatest amount of change takes place very early in therapy, then slows as the number of sessions increases. But that problem doesn't happen with BWRT because we do a simple trick that, for a moment or two, keeps exactly the same concept or idea in both conscious thought and the reptilian complex so that we can make changes at root.

Now, you could use the Stop the Clock technique you learned in Chapter 1, where you left an event frozen in the past because you are effectively stopping a sensation in its tracks. You could even use that technique for every problem but, while it's effective for relatively minor issues, it doesn't always work well for more profound situations and concepts. So we're going to create something stronger for the bigger stuff and this part of it is called Stop and Stare. It's not designed to fix anything on its own, although it is certainly one of the most vital parts of the procedure. Practice is important to learn how to use it effectively and we'll explore two different ways – for some situations one might be better than the other, but if you're only able to get on well with one of them you'll be able to use that one all the time.

For the first scenario, imagine somebody riding a bicycle in a crowded park. They're weaving between people – some of whom had to dodge out of the way – while a couple of children run along after the cyclist, giggling. (If you can't visualise it very well, think of it as if you are trying to describe your main living room to somebody who has never seen it.) Now imagine you can stop time by staring hard at the scene or by staring hard into the scene. See it as being three-dimensional – as if you could walk into it – rather than a flat picture, like a photograph. Imagine you can walk around it like a visitor; look at the expressions on the faces of the people, how they're dressed – and maybe notice somebody in the middle dodging out of the way, perhaps looking angry. Look at the cyclist: are they male or female? How do they look? Make it all as vivid in your mind as you can.

When you can do that fairly easily, try the same thing with an actual memory – something from a while ago but recent enough to be clear in your mind. Choose something pleasant that you can clearly remember for this exercise. It works best when you view it in dissociated mode – so you might be able to see yourself, though it's not a problem if not. Again, imagine you can stop time by staring at the scene. When everything is absolutely motionless and silent and neutral – because even sound has been stopped – then take in everything you can about that one tiny moment in time, while making sure that is all that is in your mind. It will take total concentration but the effort will be well worth it.

Glass Encapsulation

Here's a slightly different method of stopping an event in its tracks that's particularly recommended for some scenarios – as you will see later in the book. Again, we'll have an imaginary scene first to practise with: this time a busy office with people on phones, looking at computer screens, some bustling along with folders under their arms, others busily typing and a few in a group looking as if they're discussing something important. This time imagine that, as you stare at it, everything gradually becomes encased in a kind of glassy substance; you can then use the power of your mind to shrink it down to a cube-shaped block, small enough to pick up and move somewhere else if you wanted to.

You'll be using that technique later, but now it's time to work with the memory you decided to practise with earlier. See it as if from the outside – dissociated – and stop and stare at it until it looks as if it's frozen in one infinitesimal moment of time. You might discover that it suddenly feels different – less uncomfortable than before; this is quite normal and, in fact, the best possible response. On the other hand, you might not because this is only a part of the procedure and any changes it makes may not be permanent. There is still quite a bit to do to convince that reptilian complex that any changes are (a) desirable and (b) acceptable to the rest of the psyche. So far, all that's happened is that you've temporarily arrested the progress of the memory but you've also done something else important that you might not recognise:

> When you stop the scene and stare, you have the same thought (or image) in both the reptilian complex and your conscious thoughts for just a second or two.

It might feel longer than that – but if it does, it's evidence that it wasn't. As daft as that might sound, the fact is that the reptilian complex has no concept of time – only of what is there. As soon as you start to notice time, you're at least partly in the conscious mind. So, try again: take either of your own memories, stop time and stare at the memory with full concentration and you'll almost certainly notice that something definitely feels different. Don't worry if you don't seem to have too much luck at first, because it will get easier as you progress through the exercises in the book. You'll need to use it in slightly different ways from time to time, but once you've mastered the Stop and Stare technique you have the most important part of it. This chapter is actually one big exercise all the way through and when you've completed it you'll have the basic procedure you'll be using over and again for all sorts of issues.

Virtual Reality

This part – really a mini process in itself – is effectively the engine of the change process: a virtual reality movie in your mind consisting of:

1. The Stop and Stare scene just after it's stopped.
2. Immediately block it with the New You image.
3. Focus on the feeling in your body of the New You.
4. See a rapid flash of thousands of animated neural pathways lighting up all over the brain (it doesn't have to be anatomically accurate because you know what it represents – it can just look like a flashing network of multicoloured threads).
5. Dive into the waiting Ideal Future as the New You.
6. The Ideal Future immediately becomes active.

Text to record

To record this part of it, say the following (taking note of the pauses):

1. 'Think of the [*insert problem here*] and make it active.' (5-second pause)

2. 'And Stop and Stare the scene.' (2-second pause)

3. 'Now focus on the stopped scene, then block it quickly with the New You.'

4. 'And now notice the feeling of the New You in your body.'

5. (Fast and urgently, as though trying to make somebody sit up and take notice) 'Rapid flashes of hundreds of neurons start to light up all over the brain like a flashing network of multicoloured threads or LEDs. There are thousands of them all working perfectly and it feels so good!'

6. (Urgent) 'Now dive into the Ideal Future as the New You.'

7. (Urgent) 'And the Ideal Future becomes active like real life.'

When you get to step 7, immediately read from step 3 five more times – going as fast as you can. When you listen to it back, it should be so fast you almost can't keep up with it. Don't be tempted to slow it down because it's supposed to be difficult to follow, as odd as that sounds. Also, notice that the script uses *you* and not *me* – even though you're referring to yourself – and that's because the brain responds much better that way and all the procedures will use a similar format to this one.

After that stage, complete the Super Unwind – Part Two (see page 22) and rest for a few minutes, while concentrating on making your face as expressionless as possible. This serves as a message to the reptilian complex that you are totally at ease with everything that has gone before. Don't be tempted to skip this stage or similar on any of the procedures, since it is an essential element of the BWRT methodology. The reason for the speedy dialogue is that it's the best way of indicating urgency, and urgency is what communicates importance to that part of the brain.

There's just a little more work to do before the procedure itself with your selected mildly uncomfortable problem (you might have discovered by now that the problem you've been working on has somehow lost its bite; in which case, choose another one to practise with). So, make sure you're completely clear what it is you want to work on, then choose your two-word phrase for the New You (*relaxed* and *calm*, for example). Think of a familiar situation where you feel exactly like that, notice exactly where those feelings are in your body and create a clear mental image or thought picture in your mind. Finally, we're going to create a placeholder for your ideal future: imagine somebody in the situation you're working on – somebody who feels exactly the way you've chosen in your two-word phrase. Stop the scene, do the swap over, then come out of the scene leaving it prepared and ready.

The procedure

1. Bring the problem to mind and focus on it enough to make it feel as bad as you can, or as bad as you can handle.

2. Immediately stop it by staring hard at the worst part of it.

3. Continue into the Virtual Reality section (now ideally with your eyes closed):
    - Focus on the stopped scene and immediately replace it with the New You image.
    - Focus strongly on the feeling of the New You in your body.
    - See thousands of flashes of neural pathways lighting up in the brain.
    - Dive into the Ideal Future as the New You.
    - Zoom in to actually become the New You as the Ideal Future becomes active.

4. Repeat step 3 five more times, quickly; this is the recursive loop.

5. Drift down into the reptilian complex and concentrate on the internal universe of your mind for just a few minutes (Super Unwind – Part Two on page 22), making your face as expressionless as possible.

6. After returning to full awareness, open your eyes and bring the concept you've just worked with to mind. Check the PAL again; don't just remember it – actually feel it. If it's higher than, say, half of what it was originally, you can go through the whole procedure again (you can anyway, if you want to, since it can cause no harm). But you won't know how much you've improved the situation until you're actually in it once more.

Text to record

The text to record follows a similar format as previously and assumes you've noted the PAL of whatever you're working with:

1. 'Think of [*insert problem here*] and make it feel as bad as you can stand.' (5-second pause)

2. 'Stop it by staring hard at the worst part of it.' (2-second pause)

3. 'Now focus on that stopped scene, then block it quickly with the New You.'

4. (Quickly now) 'And now notice the feeling of the New You strongly in your body.'

5. (Fast and urgent) 'Rapid flashes of hundreds of neurons start to light up all over the brain like a flashing network of multicoloured threads or LEDs. There are thousands of them all working perfectly and it feels so good!'

6. (Urgent and intense) 'Now dive into the Ideal Future as the New You.'

7. (Urgent and intense) 'Zoom right the way into it to actually become the New You as that Ideal Future becomes active.'

Read steps 3–7 five more times, going as fast as you can. Even though it will seem very fast when you listen to it, your brain can process it (if it couldn't, you couldn't have spoken that quickly). Mistakes or stumbles are not important, so just keep going if anything like that happens. After the sixth time at step 7, continue:

8. 'Now drift down into the reptilian complex and concentrate on the internal universe of your mind, keeping your face relaxed and expressionless.'

That's the last part of the recording, and you can stay there as long as you wish – though even just one minute will be fine – and when you've come back up to full awareness, open your eyes and explore how the PAL feels. Really test it and go through the whole procedure again if it's still higher than half what it was, though – as stated previously, the real test is when you're in that troubling situation once more. And it's odds on you're in for a wonderful surprise.

That brings us to the end of this chapter. In the next one we're going to work on something that applies to everybody, even when they insist it doesn't. It addresses some of the dark corners of the human mind and delves into some very sensitive areas, because those are so often the source of anxiety – even when it doesn't feel like it. No harm will come to you if you decide to skip that one – the rest of the book is not dependent on it – but your life will improve if you take a deep breath and just dive in.

Chapter 4

The Guilty Secret – Everybody Has One

WARNING: This chapter explores sex and sexuality, along with other dark areas of the human mind, and may offend some readers in parts. It is not gratuitous, but looks at common urges, beliefs, behaviours and fears. The author was a specialist in psychosexual dysfunction for several years and achieved the Membership of the City & Guilds of London Institute (MCGI) award for his work in creating a training course on the subject for professional therapists. He was the first psychology-orientated therapist worldwide to achieve the award, which is considered equivalent to a British master's degree.

It's not unusual for an individual to totally deny they have a guilty secret. It is also not unusual, however, for them to be lying, though it's possible they don't realise that at first. To make sure you don't just simply dismiss the notion, we'll define *guilty secret* a little more clearly: in this context, it refers to anything that would be embarrassing or acutely uncomfortable if other people knew about it. Where an individual is still insistent that they are an open book and most definitely do not have anything of that sort in their life or past, there are only really three possible situations:

- They've misunderstood what is being addressed.
- They just don't care at all about what most would consider wrong or shameful.
- They are lying.

The reason is simple and we touched upon it in a previous chapter – evolution hasn't yet caught up with what is required of us in the civilised world and the human psyche still works in the way it did in our earliest human ancestors. People experience pretty much the same urges in life as those people did, including love, joy, compassion, protectiveness and other *good* drives – but those are less often the stuff of the guilty secret than the *bad* drives of jealousy, rage, desire, acquisitiveness and similar. Remember, the reptilian complex makes no such distinction as *good* or *bad*, *better* or *best* but it will recognise that shame or humiliation might be the result of some of them and suppress them when anybody is likely to observe them in action – and so the anxiety that comes from the failure to discharge an instinct gets attached to the need to keep it secret.

At this point, you might be wondering why any of this is so important. Well, it's not the secret that's the problem but the anxiety over the possibility of it being revealed. The fear of shame, punishment or humiliation is something that all but the most insensitive of individuals respond to – and this undercurrent of potential exposure can contribute to something called free-floating anxiety, which is covered in detail in Chapter 10. Whether it does so or not, or how much it does so, depends on many factors including the individual's personality, upbringing, religious views, intelligence, emotional sensitivity and more, and it would probably take an entire book on its own to catalogue every possibility. So, for the moment, just accept that if you're suffering from any form of anxiety, the thing in that dark corner of your mind just might be a contributing cause.

In this part of the book, we're going to set about making sure the past can't sabotage the future, and if it's not totally in the past but still current – well, you'll probably be able to make that feel easier as well. There is a caveat, though: the work here is designed to be used with issues and concepts that are either (a) associated with you and you alone; or (b) you were no more than 50 per cent responsible.

It is unlikely to work where there have been illegal events or where you are solely responsible for a situation which negatively affected others, though it is possible that a professional BWRT practitioner might be able to help where there is genuine remorse.

Sex and sexuality

Every living person is affected by the sex drive. Even if they are totally asexual (which is unusual) they will still be subject to comments and suggestion from others that they are in some way abnormal – so much so that they may feign normal reactions as a disguise. For the most part, once past puberty, we start to feel the urgings that are responsible for our very existence. Those urges are totally normal of course, but they can still cause problems – which is why so much anxiety is underpinned by sexuality and our response to it. Here are some of the commonest causes of difficulties associated with sex and sexuality (references to any form of illegal activity are deliberately omitted here):

- **Masturbation:** almost everybody masturbates if they are able but may feel the need to deny it because (a) it's considered sinful and forbidden by their religion; (b) they believe it's a form of self-abuse; (c) they fear it will damage their body in some way; (d) they are sure others would think them dirty; (e) they feel that it's wrong, even though they cannot say why; (f) they believe it's a form of infidelity – or that their partner does.

- **Fetish:** the real name for a fetish is a paraphilia and it refers to sexual arousal over something that, on the face of it, is just not sexy at all and may even seem gross or disgusting to others. The individual might be a millionaire genius or a homeless person – it has nothing to do with social class or intelligence – but they didn't choose to have a fetish. It's not known what causes it or why, but it's mostly in males.

- **Wild sex:** the individual who is usually sexually inhibited or unresponsive with their partner has energetic and uninhibited sexual intercourse with somebody else – possibly the legendary 'bit of rough' in which they behave as they know their partner would like them to.

- **Illicit intercourse:** the individual has had a sexual affair with somebody who was out of bounds for one reason or another (though not underage). Sex with their sibling's partner, partner's sibling or parent, close friend or employer is common.

There are many more possibilities, of course. Although the individual will not be consciously thinking about them all the time, it takes only one event where the reptilian complex perceives a risk of exposure for an anxiety response to be generated, which is possibly an attempt to trigger a physical exit from the scene.

Sometimes, if the secret is suddenly revealed, the anxiety is replaced with a sense of relief at no longer having to be watchful; at other times the despair over the sense of shame can be so profound as to trigger suicide.

Other situations

Of course, it's not only in sexual matters where there is guilt and secrecy causing difficulty but it is the category that is least sensibly talked about (use of euphemisms and coarse humour to cover embarrassment is common) and most misunderstood, so the information here might fulfil two purposes. The first is that if you identify with one of those situations listed, you can recognise that its presence is probably at least contributory to any anxiety you suffer. If it's either of the first two, the guilt is unwarranted and the exercise in this chapter will help to resolve the issue. If it's the third, the exercise will definitely be able to help – as long as you are able to accept responsibility for your part in the event, especially if it's some time in the past. If it's the fourth (or similar) it's more complicated and if the affair is still current then there's not a lot that will stop the sex drive overriding the guilt. If it's over, though – and you are genuinely remorseful – then the work later will probably help, at least to an extent.

The second purpose the information might have is where you are suffering anxiety as a result of having discovered that your partner has been involved in any of those situations. If it's either of the first two, acceptance on your part is key; if it's associated with masturbation it has no reflection on you at all. It doesn't mean they are being unfaithful or that they don't desire you – just that they had an urge for solo sex, as you probably do sometimes. Or maybe even a lot of times. If it's a fetish, they didn't choose it and might very well feel guilty about it themselves since they know that others are unlikely to understand the incessancy of the drive. If you've discovered that your partner has indulged in either wild sex or illicit intercourse though, the result might be beyond what the techniques in this book can help with (though it's definitely worth trying) and so a consultation with a professional BWRT practitioner is recommended.

Preparing your mind

In order to make what we're going to do here as effective as it can possibly be, a little mind preparation is needed. It's not complicated and might even seem very obvious – but then again it might have the effect of creating realisation, which is always a good thing. There are three important concepts to take on board:

1. Nobody ever has to know what it is you're working on; even if you were to treat yourself to a professional session or two, you wouldn't need to give the full details about anything you'd rather keep to yourself.

2. Nothing can ever be *unhappened*, however much you want it to be. You can only change the way you feel about an event in the past – you can't change it enough to totally delete it from your thoughts.

3. It's not possible to change the way that somebody else thinks or behaves (though they might change as a result of you doing so). The only person you can directly change is you – and the exercise later gives you the opportunity to do so.

Once you accept these three concepts as valid, you have a little more work to do for the exercise. Remembering the PAL from Chapter 3, where we score an event according to its severity on a scale of 1 to 10, what will you score your guilty secret as? Before you make up your mind, imagine – just for a moment – that somebody is about to make the whole thing public knowledge so that everybody knows: now decide on that PAL level. If the score is lower than 8, it's likely there's a worse secret you might be trying to keep out of your mind – but nobody other than you will know so just take a deep breath and go for it. If it's still lower than 8 then continue as long as it is genuinely the worst one you have – because if there's something there that carries more anxiety, the exercise here will almost certainly achieve little or nothing.

We're not quite ready to investigate the exercise itself yet, since there's one more decision to be made. Note whether the secret is about:

1. Something about the way you are (so you didn't choose it).

2. Something you did (or failed to do) some years ago (not within the last five years).

3. Something you still do (that doesn't cause harm or distress to another).

4. More than one of the above.

Reminder: this procedure is designed to work with personal guilt about something that has either never caused pain or distress to another, or that has 'expired' because it is more than five years old. It is unlikely to work very well, if at all, where the guilt is the result of illegal activities or where you have been solely responsible for a situation that has negatively affected others more recently than five years ago.

You will need to memorise a phrase for the Guilt Buster you will be working with shortly. To select it, choose the corresponding number that matches your response from the list above:

1. 'You didn't choose it and so it's not your fault.'

2. 'The guilt has hurt and punished you enough now.'

3. 'You know you will change that as soon as you can.'

4. 'You're already making changes today.'

It's important that you genuinely mean the phrase you choose, especially if it's (3) or (4) – BWRT doesn't work with anything that your reptilian complex knows to be untrue. There's no fooling it, so unless you truly mean what you state, the procedure will simply not work. To ensure success, say the chosen phrase out loud; if it feels good or neutral, notice where that good or neutral feeling is in the body. If, on the other hand, it feels uncomfortable it might mean that you are not admitting something to yourself, so investigate carefully and try it again. Only when you can say the phrase with a good or neutral feeling should you proceed – just repeating it a few times might help.

We're using a slightly modified procedure for the work here, so do read it through a few times (especially the Virtual Reality section) before attempting to apply it – it needs to be right all the way through to get the best out of it. It doesn't use the PAL or New You techniques (since they are not required this time), but it does still need an Ideal Future. To create that for this procedure, imagine a photograph of you being the centre of sudden unexpected attention in a crowd of people and clearly loving every moment of it (if you've never liked being the centre of attention, you're probably beginning to understand why). Whether or not you know the people you see in the imaginary photo is unimportant, but do make it so vivid it seems almost real.

The procedure is fairly long so, as previously suggested, you will probably want to read the provided text into a recorder and follow along with your eyes closed.

The Guilt Buster

1. Create an image in your mind of you involved in the secret; if it's more than one event, create an image that you know covers everything. It can be in the form of an imaginary series of images or a mental video.

2. Focus on the worst part of it and allow it to feel as uncomfortable as possible – you don't need to score it this time but do allow it to feel as bad as you can handle for just a moment.

3. Immediately Stop and Stare so that everything stops – including the guilty feeling – allowing the image to fade a little.

4. Go immediately into a modified Virtual Reality section (ideally, eyes closed now):
   - Focus on the stopped image.
   - Say your chosen phrase out loud and take a moment to notice the stopped image has faded a little more.
   - Focus on the feeling in your body as you speak the phrase.
   - See thousands of flashes of neural pathways lighting up in the brain.
   - Dive into the waiting Ideal Future.
   - The Ideal Future immediately becomes active; zoom in to become a part of it for a moment.

5. Repeat step 4 five more times as quickly as you can with urgency.

6. Drift down into the reptilian complex and concentrate on the internal universe of your mind for just a few minutes (the Super Unwind – Part Two on page 22), making your face as expressionless as possible.

7. After returning to full awareness, open your eyes and investigate that secret again. If your preparation was good and you completed the

Virtual Reality section with the image of the secret fading each time, there will be a noticeably lighter feeling.

Text to record

1. 'Make an image or a kind of mental video of you involved in the secret.' (5-second pause)

2. 'Now focus on the very worst part of it and let it feel as bad as you can bear.' (5-second pause)

3. 'Now Stop and Stare the scene so that everything stops, including the emotion, then make the image fade just a little bit.' (2-second pause)

4. 'And focus strongly on that stopped image.'

5. (Fast and urgent now) 'And recognise the truth that [*insert chosen phrase*] and notice the feeling of relief sweeping through your mind and body and as that image fades a little bit more when rapid flashes of hundreds of neurons start to light up all over the brain like a flashing network of multicoloured threads or LEDs running from front to back and side to side and it feels so good!'

6. (Urgent and intense) 'Now dive into the Ideal Future and zoom right the way into it to become an actual part of it as it suddenly becomes active.'

At this point, read steps 4–6 five more times, going as fast as you can – even though it will seem very fast when you listen to it, your brain can process it (if it couldn't, you couldn't have spoken that quickly). After the sixth time at step 6, continue:

7. 'Now drift down into that reptilian complex and concentrate on the internal universe of your mind, keeping your face relaxed and expressionless.'

That's the last part of the recording; you can stay there as long as you wish – though even just one minute will be fine – and when you've come back up to full awareness, open your eyes and explore how you feel about that guilty secret. If there's still noticeable discomfort, go through the whole thing again using a different chosen phrase if it seems relevant to do so.

All BWRT processes and procedures can be repeated as often as you like. It doesn't wear off because we're not putting anything into your mind that hasn't come from your mind in the first place. But, as with all forms of inter- vention, some people respond differently from others; some people only

need to experience the process once and their issue is resolved perma-
nently, others need another go or two to get the result they need – and only
very occasionally is any booster work needed. When this is the case, it's
usually because of something ongoing in life creating anxiety that is in
some way connected to the issue being worked on – investigation is
needed, but that's beyond the scope of this book.

In the next chapter, we're going to investigate how you can boost your
immune system to maximum efficiency.

Chapter 5

How to Boost Your Immune System

There has been much scientific research into the way the mind affects bodily systems, including how stress and anxiety can affect the immune system.[1] The science of psychoneuroimmunology[2] uses the mind–body connection to improve health and even alleviate illness. This chapter provides a simple but effective way to boost your own immunological defences. It is almost exactly the same as that used by many professional BWRT practitioners.

The procedure you are going to learn here can be used as often as you like. It can become part of a daily plan, along with anything else from this book, or you can use it whenever you think you might feel the need for it. The great thing about BWRT is that it can do no harm because the reptilian complex will just not respond to anything it perceives as intrinsically harmful, which is why we need some preparation in most procedures to ensure the replacement processes are accepted as safe. Most procedures will not need to be repeated much, if at all, but in this one we are trying to boost a natural process, rather than correct an error, and so it can be useful to repeat it as required.

---

1 J. Wolkin, Train Your Brain to Boost Your Immune System, *Mindful* [blog] (23 March 2016). Available at: https://www.mindful.org/train-brain-boost-immune-system/; American Psychological Association, Stress Weakens the Immune System, *Research in Action* [blog] (23 February 2006). Available at https://www.apa.org/research/action/immune.
2 See https://www.sciencedirect.com/topics/medicine-and-dentistry/ psychoneuroimmunology.

The immune system (looked at in medical terms) is an enormously complex network of glands, hormones, the lymphatic system, neural pathways, and the connection of all those to just about every organ in the body, including the skin. It's all looked after automatically by the autonomic nervous system and that is responsive to, and inextricably connected with, the responses from the brainstem and the reptilian complex.

This is why periods of stress are frequently followed by illness – the severity of which might depend upon the level and longevity of stress and anxiety. It's not a surprise, therefore, that people who are anxious most of the time frequently come down with anything from a minor cold all the way up to a catastrophic illness (not necessarily terminal but always something that is likely to be incurable and which irrevocably changes the client's life and lifestyle). That stress mechanism is simple: stress raises levels of cortisol, and elevated cortisol can suppress your immune system by reducing inflammation, and that in turn lowers the number of white blood cells in your blood – the lymphocytes – which fight infection. So, while the rest of this book is all about working to alleviate the various forms of psychological issues, here we're going to tune up your immune response so that you are totally equipped for the full enjoyment of life.

There is no pretence that you are going to learn to do anything that would be medically recognised, but you are going to work with every one of the basic components of the immune system:

- Thymus gland
- Adrenal glands
- Cytotoxic T cells
- Regulatory T cells
- Helper T cells

When they are all working properly together they form a fantastic weapon against infection and, by increasing their activity with the procedure you will learn here, you will create the best immune response possible. That's the reason this procedure works so well – it uses psychology and imagination to mobilise your natural bodily resources to work as efficiently as they possibly can.

Now, a bit of explanation about each of those components will help you understand them clearly enough to get the best out of your natural immune response. Cytotoxic T cells are more commonly known as killer T cells, the task of which (as their name suggests) is to destroy invaders such as bacteria and viruses. Regulatory T cells stop the killer T cells from killing bits we don't want killed (sometimes that mechanism goes wrong in auto-immune disorders and the killer cells start to attack perfectly healthy body parts instead). Finally, the helper T cells act as messengers between the basic (innate) immune system we are born with and the one that develops gradually throughout life (the acquired one) as we come into contact with all sorts of bacteria and viruses.

That leaves us with the thymus gland and adrenal glands. The thymus is under your breastbone, near the top – just a couple of inches or so down from the little hollow at the base of the front your neck. You can think of the gland as rather irregularly shaped and spongy. As far as colour is con-cerned, it changes from a greyish pink to yellow as we get older. For our work here we're going to use the *greyish pink* in the procedure. The adrenals (they often get called that slang name) sit one on top of each kidney – you can think of them as orange-coloured and triangular, about 10 mm high, 30 mm wide and 60–70 mm long. To know where they are in the body you have to know where the kidneys are, of course, and 'in my back' isn't really sufficient here. They are in your back – just below your ribcage and roughly fist-sized – with the right one being very slightly lower than the left (and, in case you're curious, that's because your liver gets in the way).

There's more to learn yet, but now it's time for a tiny practice that will stand you in good stead later on. Place the fingertips of either hand on the area of your breastbone, over the thymus; press gently, send your thoughts to the gland and see if you can be aware of it (you won't be able to actually feel it because it has no sensory nerves) while you can feel your fingers pressing against your chest. Notice the feeling because you will be doing this again later when we get to the Immune Boost procedure itself.

Connections

Now for a bit more learning. It's not quite enough to know what those immune system components are, where they are and what they do because there's a vital element that's still missing: the connection between them all. They are part of an integrated process wherein T cells – all of them – are produced mostly in the bone marrow of the pelvis. They are carried in the circulatory system to the thymus gland, which matures and conditions them into the correct proportions of *killer*, *regulatory* and *helper*. In turn, they set about attacking any invaders – creating inflammation as they do

 is sensed by the adrenal glands, which then produce more cortisol
    sol controls inflammation. This is why excessive cortisol – caused by
      s as part of the fight or flight process – can cause illness: it dampens
down the action of the immune system.

There's just one more thing you need to be aware of: the neural pathways
that connect to the thymus and adrenal glands. In both cases they come
from the spine, roughly between the upper part of your shoulder blades for
the thymus and from just above the waist for the adrenal glands.

Now another exercise: place your fingertips over the thymus, as you did
before, and imagine several nerve paths going from the spine to the gland
just beneath your fingertips. Send your thoughts to roughly where your
kidneys are – remembering the right one is very slightly lower than the left
– and think about those orange triangular adrenal glands on top. Like the
thymus, they have no sensors for you to feel them so just imagine several
nerve paths travelling from your spine to one adrenal gland, then the other.
Now the tricky bit (and don't worry if you find this difficult at first because
just the act of trying will prepare your reptilian complex for the work): with
your fingers over the thymus and pressing on your breastbone, be as aware
as you can of the gland (or even just where it is) and of the nerve paths
travelling to it from the spine; once that's in your mind, keep it there while
you send your thoughts to the adrenal glands and the nerve paths to each
one of those from the spine.

Yes, that is a difficult exercise at first. But it doesn't have to be perfect and
if the best you can manage is to rapidly – very rapidly – switch your
thoughts between each stage, all will work perfectly well later. If you cannot hold them all at once, it might come out as something like:

1. Fingertips on thymus with awareness.
2. Nerve paths to thymus.
3. Thoughts to adrenals.
4. Nerve path to first adrenal gland.
5. Nerve path to second adrenal gland.
6. Repeat steps 1–5 several times quickly.

It's a good idea to become familiar and at ease with that preparation
because it's used in the full procedure, coming up shortly. We're taking a
slightly different approach this time since the focus is going to be on your
internal body systems, rather than on the way you fit into the world. There

won't be a PAL, a New You or the Ideal Future in this version since, not only are they not necessary, they would simply get in the way of the process. You'll be working as if observing your immune system from the outside, but also switching to whatever physical awareness you can manage – and the stronger that aspect of it all is, the better. But if the best you can manage is just thinking of that awareness without actually feeling it, the whole procedure will still work almost as well. The reason why it would be only almost as well is that not being able to find that physical awareness means that you currently have not developed that part of your system. But if you are able to feel the awareness you can now just skip to the Immune Boost (see page 50).

Okay, you're still here – so a little practice might help. Imagine you are sending a thought to your left big toe and become aware of it. You were almost certainly not aware of it until this very moment but you probably are aware of it now. Do the same thing with the back of your right knee, then your left shoulder and now your lower lip. There may have been a feeling in each of those places, or you were just aware of them – either way this is exactly what we need. Now think of your stomach – the inside, not the outside – and, again, if there's a feeling or just an awareness it's absolutely fine. The reason why these places are easier to find is simply that you are more familiar with them than you are the thymus and adrenal glands, especially if you have never really thought about them, or where they are, before now.

The thymus is the easiest gland to find awareness of, so we'll focus on that one first. Press your fingertips against the breastbone – just a couple of inches down from the little hollow at the base of your neck, as before (you did do that before, didn't you?), and be aware of what you can feel. Now think of the thymus gland itself just an inch or two away but directly in line with your fingertips on the other side of the breastbone. Remove your fingertips and search to see if you still have some awareness of that whole area – if it feels as if you can only be aware of where your fingers were pressing, that'll work just as well.

The adrenal glands are a little more difficult because it's not easy to place your fingertips over them, so instead first think of your spine a couple of inches above your waist (and you can place your fingertips there if you want to). Imagine nerve threads running out from there towards each side, then imagine them connecting into the orange triangular-shaped glands on top of the kidney on either side, one at a time. If you can become aware of only the outside of your back on both sides, that will be very nearly as good as if you can feel some sort of awareness of the glands themselves – the reptilian complex will sense your intent.

If you're still not sure, practice will improve things – but if you really cannot find that awareness, don't let it put you off. If you can understand where the glands are then you will still get more benefit from doing the procedure than from not doing it.

Immune Boost

Please note: this one definitely should be recorded since you're working at a very complex issue and you need to be totally relaxed to get the best from it. As usual, the text to record is given after the outline of the procedure.

1. Imagine you can see yourself as if from the outside and you can see those glands and nerve paths, seeing the colours as pale to begin with: a faint pink for the thymus and its nerves; a faint orange for the adrenals and their nerves.

2. Search to feel whatever awareness you can find; if you can't find awareness, it's okay because the search will send the message.

3. Now imagine you can see them suddenly becoming visibly active – maybe with pulses like tiny pale-coloured LEDs running rapidly along the nerve paths – and the glands themselves gently pulsing. Try to see it in your mind's eye but it's okay if you can't because just trying will send the right message. Now continue with that pattern you practised a little while ago:

4. Fingertips on thymus with awareness.

5. Nerve paths to thymus from upper spine.

6. Thoughts to adrenals.

7. Nerve path to first adrenal gland from middle spine.

8. Nerve path to second adrenal gland from middle spine.

9. See the pink of the thymus becoming stronger (each time).

10. See the orange of the adrenal glands becoming stronger (each time).

11. The nerve paths and the glands are still gently pulsing.

12. Remove your fingertips, then replace them quickly.

13. Repeat steps 4–12 five more times as fast as you can – 20 seconds per cycle or faster will be perfect.

14. The thymus and adrenal glands and their nerve paths are now vibrant and healthily active.

15. Drift down into the reptilian complex and concentrate on the internal universe of your mind for just a few minutes (the Super Unwind – Part Two on page 22), making your face as expressionless as possible.

16. After returning to full awareness, open your eyes and briefly visualise the thymus and adrenal glands looking healthy. This last step is essentially a belt and braces approach to confirm the change.

Text to record

This procedure is longer than those covered so far – it's the longest one in the whole book, in fact – so it's a good idea to practise the text a few times before recording it. This one needs to be fairly clear in the places where you're asking for a physical response.

1. 'Imagine you can see yourself and look at where the thymus gland is and where the adrenal glands are and imagine the nerve paths as well as you can with the colours pale to begin with. Think of a faint pink for the thymus and its nerves and a faint orange for the adrenals and their nerves.' (10-second pause)

2. 'Now search to see if you can feel something for the thymus and adrenals.' (10-second pause)

3. 'See or imagine those nerves becoming active with pulses like tiny LEDs running along the nerve paths and the glands themselves gently pulsing.' (5-second pause)

4. 'Now put your fingertips on the thymus position.'

5. 'Be aware of the feeling in your fingers and the thymus.'

6. 'Think of the nerves from your spine to the thymus.'

7. 'Now think of the adrenals and the nerves from the spine to the first adrenal and then to the second adrenal.'

8. 'See the pink of the thymus becoming stronger and see the orange of the adrenals becoming stronger.'

9. 'Look at the nerve paths and glands and see them still gently pulsing.'

10. 'Lift your fingers then put them back really quickly.'

Now repeat steps 5–10 really quickly, five more times – if you can do it in 20 seconds for each cycle that will be perfect. Then continue:

11. 'The thymus and adrenals now look healthy and vibrantly active and you can let your arms relax as you drift down into that reptilian complex and concentrate on the internal universe of your mind, keeping your face relaxed and expressionless.'

As usual, that's the last part of the recording and you can stay there as long as you wish – though even just one minute will be fine – and when you've come back up to full awareness, open your eyes again.

With this routine there's nothing to check, since it's sufficient just to complete the procedure – your body will do as well as it is able. When you've become used to this one, you'll be able to run it in just a few moments without the recording (experience will let you do it in as little as two or three minutes) whenever you wish, and you could include it in the weekly plan (see page 175). Now you're ready for the next chapter, where you'll learn how to make major changes for yourself.

Chapter 6

Preparing for Major Changes

If we want major changes to stick and not just run out of steam after a few days or weeks, we have to look at a few underlying thought processes – and the work you've done already will have made that task a lot easier. That's still true, even if you decide in a little while that what you're reading in this chapter doesn't really apply to you, because the more you understand about the way the reptilian complex does its work, the more physical access to that part of your psyche you are creating.

It's very likely that you'll recognise most of the thought processes discussed here straight away though, and one or two may even irritate you a little at first. That's especially going to be the case if you know that most, or all, of your problems are because of something – or lots of somethings – that happened in your past. But even if that's the case (and it quite possibly is) there is still a fundamental truth to take on board: it doesn't matter who did what to you, or when, nor how often they repeated it; the only person who can sort it out is you.

That sounds easier said than done, of course. What you are learning here makes it possible, but there is a catch (you knew there would be): you have to actually want to let go of the resentfulness, anger, hate, sadness, hurt or whatever it is you feel about what happened. Those are non-productive negative emotional responses that do nothing at all for you, except compromise your psychological and physical health far more than you might realise. We need to make as much use of the positive power in your mind as possible for the work in this chapter, rather than giving some of it away to people who have not behaved well towards you.

You might not have realised until this very moment that those who hurt you still have a hold over you. They only have to come into your thoughts for any reason at all to trigger those negative feelings that can actually physically weaken you, even if you're not totally aware of it at the time. And it's that that's not fair.

Of course, you might at this moment be thinking something like: 'Nobody did anything to me at all, it's just the way I am.' Well, we're born knowing nothing of the world and we're all pretty much equal at that point in our lives. So, if you now find yourself to be anxious, depressed, low on self-worth, struggling with performance anxiety of any sort, suffering from phobias or anything else, it's because you've learned it. And that means somebody taught you, even if you can't remember who that was or even if you're certain that this is not the case. So, in this chapter, you'll be working with one of two situations:

- You know that your problems are caused by the way you were treated by others and it makes you angry, sad or some other negative emotional response.
- You don't really know why you have your problems, but you think it's probably just the way you are and not because of what anybody else said or did.

Whichever one applies to you, do read both the following sections; you might well be surprised to discover that some parts of each seem to find a definite relevance in your mind.

Somebody else did it

It doesn't matter if whoever you are thinking of was downright hateful and aggressively determined to cause as many problems as possible, or whether they were just not very capable and made loads of mistakes that caused huge problems. It really isn't important how they were because if you feel that they were the cause of your problems, then they were – even if they didn't know it. There could be a difficulty in that you might not be prepared to let them off – you might want to show them what they've done to you or somehow pay them back or give them a taste of their own medicine. Even if you were to find a way of doing that, though, it would not change anything – not for very long, anyway. There might be a fleeting satisfaction at the time but the fact is that whatever they did would remain done and cannot ever be undone. The response to whatever they did is still in that reptilian complex of yours and it's there that change must be made.

We'll look at how to do that later but, as you've already read, you have to want that change – otherwise you're very likely to get in your own way and sabotage the entire process.

If you're struggling with that idea, you might be trapped by hate – one of the most damaging emotions. But the thing is, if the *hatee* deserves it, they probably don't care – and if they do care, they probably don't deserve it (however much it feels to you that they do). The biggest problem about hate is that it tends to turn inwards because it can never truly be discharged, and when an instinct cannot be discharged it creates anxiety. So it's impossible to be happy when you carry hate in your psyche – the reptilian complex can never let you be at ease in case the object of your hate suddenly appears in your life.

Effectively then, you have two choices: (a) decide that there is no way at all you are ever going to let go of the feelings you harbour and you're at ease with continuing just as you are; or (b) decide that although what happened wasn't fair, it still gives them a hold over you and you'll disempower them at the first opportunity.

If you've determinedly decided on (a), then you probably feel as if you'd be letting them off, rather than taking power back from them. There's no criticism here because, as you know now, you cannot control your feelings – only what you do with them, and you're allowed to decide what that is. If, on the other hand, you've decided on the second choice – to remove yourself from their malign influence – then you'll have the tools to make a real difference very shortly.

If you've decided on (a) the rest of this chapter might hold little interest for you, but it's a good idea to read it anyway so that you are in as full possession of every relevant fact as possible. You might decide to reverse your decision, though there will be no attempt to persuade you in that direction.

Nobody else did it

The important thing here is that whatever problem you are experiencing, it's there for a reason – even if that sounds like nonsense. But you didn't have it when you were born, so that reptilian complex of yours has adopted it – whatever it is – for one reason or another. Most symptoms are either based in anxiety or cause anxiety under certain circumstances; an example would be social phobia which causes anxiety if you think you might have to go to a social event or a restaurant, for instance. It might well feel as if the anxiety is the cause of the problem, but it can just as easily be the other way round: that the symptom, whatever it is, is designed to keep you away from some situation or another that the reptilian complex has learned is unsafe for you, if not for others.

So, essentially, whatever symptom you suffer provides some sort of benefit – and if that benefit includes getting you attention of some sort (which it almost certainly does, though it might or might not be important to you), then you have a choice to make: (a) decide to stay as you are and continue to get the attention from those who may view you as somebody who doesn't cope with life very well; or (b) decide to fix the whole thing and get even more attention by being an inspiration to others. If you chose (a), there may be nothing else in this chapter that is of interest to you but it would still be a good idea to read it anyway. You never know – it might be one of the best decisions you've made in your entire life.

The core

Maybe you're sure you know exactly what lies at the root of your psychological difficulties, but the truth is that if you did know, you would be able to solve the problem. Anxiety, depression, poor self-worth, absent self-confidence and just about everything else are usually the result of the cause, rather than the cause itself. If you knew exactly what that cause was, you could take steps to fix it. It doesn't matter if it's something from so long ago it's out of date, because, as mentioned before, that bit of the brain doesn't *do* time – it just responds to whatever is there – and if it viewed something as out of bounds once, it probably still does. One thing is absolutely for certain – it's not just the way you are. It never is. There will always be a core event or concept at the root of it all.

That core can be caused by our expectations of – and from – life, and usually is; there's rather more to those than you might ever have realised. Although it sounded far-fetched not so long ago, many psychologists now subscribe to the notion of the *collective unconscious*.[1] This is not a spiritual or psychical thing, as you might at first believe, but the idea that we are born with inherited expectations of how life should be. C. G. Jung first

---

1 The Editors of Encyclopaedia Britannica, Collective Unconscious, *Encyclopedia Britannica* (28 February 2020). Available at: https://www.britannica.com/science/collective-unconscious.

proposed this idea in 1928,[2] suggesting that the collective unconscious holds mental patterns, or memory traces, which are shared with all other humans and to which we all respond. His work is too complex for the non-psychologist to properly understand, never mind work with, but there are elements that stand up to close investigation and which suit our purpose here.

Translated to our modern world, Jung's concept would be seen as what might be called ancestral memory passed on from one generation to the next via RNA (a companion molecule to DNA) – a concept that has been confirmed by much research.[3] What this means in this context is that situations that are repeated over many generations create an inherited instinct in the reptilian complex that this is how life should be. The problem is that these expectations were based on a world very different from the one in which we live today, and for most people it is all but impossible that they could ever be met. Jung proposed a dozen *primary archetypes*[4] – each one associated with different aspects of life and living – but we're only interested in two, since one or both are so often the core of an individual's issues. Those two are the *mother* and the *father* and for our purposes we can consider the inherited expectations to be comparable to these concepts:

- Mother is the nurturer and teacher whose task is to ensure the child safely reaches maturity, is able to understand the world and function competently and safely.

- Father is the protector, tasked with ensuring safety from all harm, guiding the child on how to look after itself effectively and function competently and safely.

These are not Jung's description of those archetypes (he was not so succinct by a long shot) but so many people feel in some way let down by their

2   C. G. Jung, *Collected Works of C.G. Jung, Volume 9 (Part 1): The Archetypes and the Collective Unconscious*, ed. H. Read, M. Fordham and G. Adler, tr. R. F. C. Hull. (Abingdon and New York: Routledge, 2014 [1959]).
3   I. Lacal and R. Ventura. Epigenetic Inheritance: Concepts, Mechanisms and Perspectives. *Frontiers in Molecular Neuroscience* 11 (2018): 292. Available at: https://www.frontiersin. org/articles/10.3389/fnmol.2018.00292/full; N. P. F. Kellermann, Epigenetic Transmission of Holocaust Trauma: Can Nightmares be Inherited? *Israel Journal of Psychiatry and Related Sciences* 50(1) (2011): 33–37; J. L. Kwapis and M. A. Wood, Epigenetic Mechanisms in Fear Conditioning: Implications for Treating Post-Traumatic Stress Disorder. *Trends in Neurosciences* 37(12) (2014): 706–720; D. Treffert, Genetic Memory: How We Know Things We Never Learned, *Scientific American* [blog] (28 January 2015). Available at https://blogs. scientificamerican.com/guest-blog/genetic-memory-how-we-know-things-we-never-learned.
4   Jung, *Collected Works of C. G. Jung, Volume 9 (Part 1)*.

parents that they make sense. It's logical also from the practical viewpoint of the way parents should behave and mirrors the natural instincts of most animals, other than humans. But their children only demand nurture and protection, just as human children did – until relatively recently. Our modern materialistic and acquisitive world, though, is totally different from that of other animals and evolution moves only slowly, so it will be many thousands of years yet before it catches up. If it ever does. Also, the roles of modern parents have become blurred and one or the other might have to be away for extended periods for their career, or maybe they divorce and one of them has to attempt to fulfil both roles. But because evolution does move so slowly, they have not yet inherited the instincts of the other role.

Now, here's a simple scenario that illustrates the problem:

- Child 1 has rich parents who buy him an iPad to keep him out of their way while they get on with work or their own hobbies. He is happy with his possession.

- Child 2 has parents who are loving but not rich. She perceives the iPad as highly desirable and wants one, but her parents can't afford it. She feels deprived.

It's not important in this scenario that Child 1 was deprived of love but it is important that Child 2 was loved but felt deprived. To her, being loved was so normal she didn't notice it – it was normal and nothing special. To her, her parents not buying her an iPad resulted in her feeling as if she was missing out. Child 1, on the other hand, didn't even know what love was and, since you cannot easily see it, did not have the feeling of being deprived. Another example will clarify further:

- Adult 1 is the product of a rich but aloof family who gave him everything he wanted. He can only measure the value of relationships by what others will give him. When anybody wants anything from him, he feels incapable and stressed.

- Adult 2 is the product of a poor family but who loved her, even when she threw tantrums about not being able to have what she wanted. She still feels as if she was deprived but values being loved, and able to love, in relationships.

Of course, you can poke holes in those stories if you try hard enough. But they are designed to illustrate something you've already read about: you cannot choose what you feel, only what you do with what you feel. They also demonstrate that what you feel might not be related to the truth, but it's still what you feel. If you feel that either or both parents let you down in some way, that feeling is valid – even if the facts are that your parents did the very best they were able for you. Now, there is the vaguest possibility that last statement has irritated or angered you, but there's no suggestion of letting them off here or making excuses for them – just the notion that what you saw and felt might be completely different from what they saw and felt. Nobody is saying you are wrong in what you believe, only that they might not have known they were.

Of course, you might be one of the lucky ones who just knows that your parents were wonderful, loving and supportive human beings. But since you're reading this book, your life is not as you would like it to be; somewhere along the line something happened to mess it up. But one solid concept is worthy of repeat: you are the only one who can sort it out.

The first thing that really needs to change, therefore, is you. Stop blaming all that's wrong on whoever you think caused it, because that just takes control away from you and makes it less likely that you will ever find the sort of life you want. Be like the professional who is called in to sort out the problem that some unskilled individual created. Take charge of the situation and do all that you can to fix it and get the best life you can. We're going to use two different procedures here and you can do either or both as you wish. The first one is for when you feel there are so many issues from childhood that the whole period needs adjusting. The second one is useful where there are one or two specific situations that you feel are at the root of everything: a sibling who was favoured, for instance; your parents splitting up; being adopted; or just something that distresses you, even though you have no idea why. The fact is that whatever the cause, it's in the past and cannot be unhappened, so the only thing you can do is change your response to it.

Childhood reissued

You're going to use the Virtual Reality process here that you experimented with in previous chapters. The first step is to conjure up an image of how somebody might look and behave if they had had the perfect childhood. How would you know that? How would they look? How would that feel, do you think? It might be someone you know or a completely imaginary person; either way make that image as vivid as you can.

Now imagine, just for a moment (longer if you can manage it), how you would be if you'd had the perfect childhood for you. Ignore what it was;

concentrate on how you would be if you had been brought up knowing that you could tackle anything and if it went wrong it was no big deal – you would just give it another shot or do something different. Imagine how it would feel to know that you were a properly developed and confident person who could do the things you believe most people do. Change things about the idea until they feel just right for you and you can imagine how you would look. This is the Best You image (you can always go back to the first image for a reminder, if necessary).

Once you have that image securely created, you can have a practice run before doing the work proper: get an image of you in your mind as you are now; the one that was stopped from developing into your best self. Now imagine you can turn the light off so that everything is completely dark. Then turn the light on again and you can suddenly see the Best You looking absolutely alive and fantastic. Do this a few times quite quickly until it's easy. Now we're almost ready to do the Virtual Reality process, but first bring that image to mind of you as you are now – and Stop and Stare so that everything is completely motionless. Remember that each step of the procedure must be done at speed, because speed is the language of urgency the reptilian complex understands. You should try to get six repeats in one minute, making sure you see every frame.

The procedure

1. Focus on the Stop and Stare image.

2. Turn the lights off and wait 1 second.

3. Turn the lights on and see the Best You image.

4. Zoom right in to actually become the Best You in your thoughts.

5. See thousands of flashes of neural pathways lighting up all over the brain.

6. The Best You immediately becomes active and you can feel it all over your body, from head to toe and fingertip to fingertip.

7. Repeat steps 1–6 six times.

8. Drift down into the reptilian complex and the Super Unwind – Part Two (see page 22).

As usual, you can stay there as long as you wish – though even just one minute will be fine – and when you've come back up to full awareness, open your eyes. There's no PAL to test this time but you can check to see how good that Best You feels; almost certainly, wonderful!

Text to record

1. 'Think of you the way you are now and Stop and Stare so that everything is completely still.' (5-second pause)

2. 'Now focus on the stopped image and make it really sharp.' (2-second pause)

3. 'And now turn the lights off.' (1-second pause)

4. 'Turn the lights on and see the Best You image looking really good.'

5. 'As you zoom right in to actually become the Best You, imagine thousands of flashes of neural pathways lighting up all over your brain.'

6. 'Now the Best You becomes active and animated and you can feel it all over your body from head to toe and fingertip to fingertip.'

Repeat steps 2–6 five more times, speaking quickly and urgently all the time, then continue with:

7. 'Now drift down into the reptilian complex into the Super Unwind – Part Two.'

Now complete the standard ending of the procedure, as at the bottom of the procedure description.

Specific Issues

Now we'll look at how to deal with specific events and issues using the longer procedure from Chapter 3 – it needs no modification of any sort. Prepare the relevant New You exactly as in Chapter 3 (see page 26): create your two-word phrase, think of a familiar situation where you feel like that and locate where in your body you feel it. Now create the Ideal Future – again, exactly as in Chapter 3 (see page 27) where you change places with somebody else. From there, run the procedure exactly as in Chapter 3 – here's a reminder, with less text this time. Slightly modified versions of this procedure will be used for the different issues covered in this book.

1. Bring whatever you're working on to mind and focus on it enough to make it feel as bad as you can, or as bad as you can handle, and get the PAL.

2. Immediately Stop and Stare the worst part of it.

3. Continue into the Virtual Reality section (now ideally with your eyes closed):
    - Focus on the Stop and Stare image.
    - Immediately replace it with the New You image.
    - Focus on the feeling of the New You in your body.
    - See thousands of flashes of neural pathways lighting up all over the brain.
    - Dive into the waiting Ideal Future as the New You.
    - The Ideal Future immediately becomes active; zoom in to actually become the New You.

4. Repeat step 3 five more times.

5. Drift down into the reptilian complex and the Super Unwind – Part Two (see page 22).

After returning to full awareness, open your eyes, bring the concept you've just worked with to mind and check the PAL again. If it's still at 4 or above, run the procedure up to two more times – any more and you're unlikely to see much improvement on this occasion, but you can run it again the next day.

Text to record

1. 'Think of [*insert problem here*] and make it as bad as it can get or as bad as you can bear and get the PAL.' (5-second pause)

2. 'Now Stop and Stare it to completely freeze it so it's absolutely stopped.' (2-second pause)

3. 'Focus on that frozen image and immediately replace it with the New You.'

4. (Fast and urgently from now on) 'Focus on the feeling of the New You in your body.'

5. 'And feel the feeling of the New You in your body as thousands of flashes of neural pathways begin to light up all over your brain.'

6. 'Now dive into the Ideal Future as the New You and as the Ideal Future straight away becomes active zoom right in to actually become the New You.'

Repeat steps 3–6 five more times quickly and urgently throughout, then continue:

7. 'Now drift down into the reptilian complex into the Super Unwind – Part Two.'

That's the end of the recording; after returning to full awareness open your eyes, bring the problem to mind and check the PAL again. If it's still at 4 or above, run the procedure up to two more times – as mentioned earlier, any more than that and you're unlikely to see much improvement, but you can run it again the next day or any other time.

That brings us to the end of Chapter 6. Next we're going to work on a specific problem that blights the lives of a great number of people.

Chapter 7

How to Boost Your Self-Worth

To an extent, Chapter 7 is *Chapter 6 – Part Two* and aimed with more precision at the problem of low self-worth. Many people don't know exactly what poor self-worth means and might only think they have it because somebody told them so. It can easily be confused with a lack of self-confidence or inferiority complex and, although there are similarities, they are certainly not the same thing. The good news is that the work in this chapter will be effective in all three cases for most people. We'll start with a look at each situation:

- Low self-worth, or low self-esteem, is a belief or feeling of being of less importance in the world than most others.
- Lack of self-confidence is a belief or feeling of not being able to do things as well as they should be done.
- Inferiority complex is a feeling of general inadequacy based on a self-perceived inability in one specific sphere of activity – having a speech impediment like a stutter or stammer, for example – even though other people might not consider the individual with such a problem to be inferior.

The only one of the three that might actually be provable is inferiority complex. Sometimes, as in the example, it's based on a reality where there really is a lack of ability in one area of life that most people handle comfortably; that awareness creates a belief of general inferiority and, quite often, a tendency to belligerent anger. It creates the fear of being thought inadequate by others and that they might then be automatically dismissive

– followed by an unshakeable belief that this is definitely the case. Hence the anger. But when it's based on something that is not obvious, or even maybe just imagined, it shares something with the other two situations – a comparison is being made between how the individual feels and how other people look.

There is one situation with poor self-worth where you might need more professional help than this chapter can give you (though it can still make an improvement) and the answer to this simple question will reveal if that is the case: if you knew for certain that you had exactly what you believe others have, no more and no less, would you still have that low self-worth? If the answer is yes, then it might be the case that something rather more powerful than the procedure in this chapter is needed; that said, it might still make at least a dent in the problem.

So, the work here is all about seeking to create enlightenment and under-standing, after which we will be employing the BWRT processes to create some rapid reorganising of the associated neural pathways in the reptilian complex. It's important to remember that the enlightenment and under-standing must come first, though, or the BWRT part of the process might not be very effective. It's possible, even likely, that you might want to argue the point in a couple of places – if so, that's just your reptilian complex trying to avoid change. After all, if you manage to raise your sense of self-worth to what you might think other people have, you might have to start behaving like other people do – the very thing your reptilian complex seeks to prevent you from doing.

We have a bit of preparation work to get through before we start and although the work is based around poor self-worth, the preparation is especially relevant to feelings of inferiority and low confidence in all its forms. The first part is to carefully explore the idea that the only real reason you are suffering from low self-worth is because you are comparing how you feel with how others seem to be. The actual feeling of low self-worth is valid, of course, because – as you already know – you cannot control what you feel. But if whatever that feeling is based on is not true, then it's fake news. It might seem that almost everybody else is more confident, more capable, more at ease – and the rest. However, all you're seeing is what they choose to let people see, which is what they want people to see. But guess what? Some of them might be lying. They might actually believe they're a big fat fake but can't bear others to know, so they do their best to keep their truth hidden. They might even be suffering from low self-worth, in fact, and you would probably be surprised to discover just how many people suffer that very problem.

It's entirely possible, of course, that you don't consciously compare yourself with anybody at all. Perhaps you can't bear even the idea of it in case your worst fears are realised and you discover proof that you truly are just an inferior being. Instead, it's something you just 'know', though you'd be hard-pressed to explain to anybody exactly how you know. You might even be so convinced of it that you're beginning to feel irritated at the suggestion here that it might possibly not be genuine. But the inescapable fact is that when you were born, you were pretty much the same as everybody else is at that point in their life. Equal. Then you started to learn straight away how you fit in to the world and what the world – which at that point is your immediate family – thinks of you. It's an inherited process that you have no control over; the collective unconscious that you read about in Chapter 6 ensures that all creatures unquestioningly accept that their elders know everything. In general, that works well because the elders know how to survive and ensure that their progeny learn the ropes so that they know how to survive and eventually pass that knowledge on to their own children. It's an inherited trait that has been passed on from generation to generation for millions of years, becoming stronger and more entrenched with the passage of time.

But where many animals teach their offspring what they have to do to survive – whether it's to hunt, fly, run, hide, freeze or whatever has got them to where they are now – the human animal does something different. We still pass on what we learned from our parents but a lot of the time, instead of what to do to survive, it's all about what not to do if we want to avoid punishment. Much of it is unavoidable, of course. We live in a sophisticated (which means false, by the way) society with all manner of social requirements and moral codes that are certainly not instinctive; we are taught to be so ashamed of some bodily functions that we have to go into a special room to perform them, and we sometimes learn to be so embarrassed of the very function that created us in the first place (along with almost all life) that we might sometimes have difficulty in performing it – perhaps even experiencing disgust. And not just with ourselves but with others as well. In the society in which we live, all of these things (and more) can be thought of as the side effects of necessary upbringing. There are more rules, of course – many of them concerned with what we must not do: don't interrupt when others are speaking, don't talk with your mouth full, don't eat with your mouth open, don't answer back, don't look at me like that,

– well, you get the idea. There are just as many *do* rules too, but they are not where the problems originate. The problems come from one of two entirely different situations:

- The parents (or parent figures) who constantly criticise, humiliate, ridicule and harangue, determined to teach the same proper values and resilience they were taught (though they might not recognise that, instead just behaving instinctively).

- The parents (or parent figures) who want their child to be among the most successful people in the world, setting the same impossibly high goals their parents set them and expressing disappointment, or maybe anger, when those targets are not met – perhaps in case it reflects badly on them as parents.

The first of those two groups take every opportunity to make sure the child understands they are dim, half-witted, slow, idiotic, a waste of space, stupid, missing a bit, weird and any other derogative term that comes to mind. The child grows up and might well recognise that none of that is actually true but the reptilian complex has already learned the self-identity and the conscious recognition makes no difference. The individual compares how others who have not experienced the criticism and ridicule appear and decides those are the proper people and how *they* are supposed to be. They already *know* they can't manage it, of course, and realise they are far less capable in the world than those others.

The second group have usually failed to reach the goals their parents set them and so believe they must be valuable aspirational targets. 'I want you to have a better life than me,' the parents declare, urging the child to work really hard to reach those targets and expressing great disappointment at any failure. One of two things happens: (1) the child grows up knowing they are a disappointment to their elders because they fail to reach important goals, compares themselves with others who appear to be at ease with themselves and sinks into the belief that they are worth less to the world than those others; or (2) if they did manage to reach the goal, they become an avid perfectionist who must cross every *t* and dot every *i* several times to avoid the possibility of whatever the parents have said would happen in the result of a fail. They see others making little apparent effort and decide they are obviously less capable than those who manage to do things so easily.

Hopefully you've identified at least partly with one of those childhood situations and are now considering that it might well be the source of your problems, as far as your sense of self is concerned. But don't rush off to punish your parents just yet because it's highly likely that they didn't set out to create the you that you have become; they probably didn't even think of it, in fact, and have not the remotest idea that they did anything untoward. They were following the urges of their reptilian complex – the origins of which were as invisible to them as the truth that you are comparing yourself with others was to you. You might have even had the baffling situation where each parent had completely different ideas about how and what you should be taught about life and the world, and that can create all manner of psychological conflict which certainly doesn't help matters. But remember, as you've already read, it doesn't matter who caused the problem or why – you are the only one who can sort it out. We've got a bit more exploration to do first though.

My parents were wonderful

If you were lucky enough to have wonderful parents who nurtured and supported you while you were learning what life was about – picking you up if you fell, encouraging you through fails, praising your successes and ensuring you had the confidence to grab every opportunity that presented itself – it's a bit of a surprise that you're reading this part of the book. Still, if you do have low self-worth there will definitely be a cause and it might even be because your parents were so wonderful; it might mean that you never discovered how to be resilient or independent, being over-nurtured all the way with somebody always ready to stand you up when you fell down and shield you from much of the common rubbish of life – protecting you from the put-downs, criticisms, mickey-taking and other personal slights that we all receive now and again. Or perhaps they taught you that you are special and the problem is that others seem not to realise this, so are dismissive or unkind towards you. Maybe, even, you had some of the richer trappings of life that others can only dream of, and they're jealous enough to make snide remarks that you might not always understand – so you feel as if you're just not as savvy as they are; definitely lacking in some important common knowledge that everybody else has.

But then again, maybe your self-worth issue didn't come from your parents at all. Maybe it was your grandparents, or an uncle or aunt. Perhaps it was an employer, the postman, or the smart alec next-door neighbour with a gazillion awards, half-a-dozen degrees and a body sculpted to perfection. It makes no difference – you've got it and we'll be fixing it very shortly.

Everybody is equal?

There are many people who will tell you that in fact everybody is equal; that we are all the same under the skin. But frankly, that's rubbish. Some are cleverer, some are athletic, some are couch potatoes, some are richer, some are poorer, some are more street-smart, some are crooked – that list could go on and on. But the important thing is that nobody is out there on their own. However you are, you can guarantee there are many, many millions around the world who are just like you. You don't see them for the same reason they don't see you: you don't push yourself forward because you know there's not really any point. You avoid situations where people might ask you what you think because you'd look like an idiot when you misunderstand. You might even acquire the reputation of being unsociable (not anti-social, which is a quite different thing) but that's a safe situation so it won't bother you. In fact, the less contact you have to make, the safer you feel. Until now, though, this might all have been completely invisible to your conscious mind.

Now, here's an interesting question: if you knew beyond doubt that they were just the same as you (not that you were just the same as them, which we looked at earlier) – that they were no cleverer, no more insightful and no more confident, would you still be just as anxious when spending time with them? The answer is probably no because you would not feel under threat. And that, in case you still needed it, is evidence of what you read earlier in this chapter – you're comparing yourself with others and usually coming off worse. So now we'd better get on to how to sort it all out.

Preparation

We're going to use a word list in a similar way to that in Chapter 3, but this time we'll be using only one list, instead of two. Choose the two phrases from the list that are the most important to you without wondering what anybody else might think. In other words, choose the two attributes that you want – it's of enormous importance that you do exactly that, without asking anybody else for their advice on what would be best for you. Here's the list:

- Personal confidence
- Attractiveness
- Feeling grown up
- Feeling equal to others

- Just doing stuff
- Not caring what others think
- Just fitting in
- Feeling others' acceptance
- Feeling a real part of things
- Seeing others as equal

When you've chosen your two phrases, making sure they really are what you want most, join them together with *and*, *because*, *from* or whatever else fits. Here are some examples of the complete phrase you'll use as the key to the New You (as in Chapter 3, page 26):

- 'attractiveness from personal confidence'
- 'just doing stuff and not caring what others think'
- 'personal confidence from just fitting in'
- 'feeling equal to others because of just doing stuff'
- 'feeling a real part of things by seeing others as equal'

Finally, adjust the phrase as necessary to fit into this part of a sentence: '... looking for all the world as though you [*insert complete phrase*] as if it's always been that way.' For instance, taking the last phrase, you would adjust it to: '... looking for all the world as though you are *feeling a real part of things by seeing others as equal* as if it's always been that way.' It's important that (a) the phrase makes proper sense; and (b) it fits sensibly into that sentence (which will be part of the procedure). Taking the first phrase now, you would have: '... looking for all the world as though you have an *attractiveness from personal confidence* that feels as if it's always been that way.' As long as you keep the phrase itself intact, all will be well – so you can add words either side to personalise it and make it yours. An example of a bit more expansion on that second phrase is: '... looking as though you have a *wonderful attractiveness from personal confidence that others notice* as if it's always been that way.' Do remember, though, that getting too complicated can make it more difficult to understand.

Next, think of a situation – we'll call it the Assessment Event – which would give you real difficulty and give it a PAL of between 1 and 10, where 10 is highest in terms of discomfort. If it's lower than 8, choose something else that does make you truly uncomfortable and anxious. If you're stuck for ideas, imagine you are required to talk about yourself and your life so far, for 15 minutes, to a group of people who are as you believe most people to be: supremely confident and worldly wise.

Finally, create the Ideal Future, and you can do that exactly as in Chapter 3 (see page 27). Imagine a lively scene where somebody is involved in a situation similar to the Assessment Event but bigger, more important and with more people involved. See them looking totally at ease – they not only look relaxed but as if they're enjoying themselves immensely and they clearly have all the attributes you've chosen in your New You phrase. Now Stop and Stare the scene so that there's not the tiniest trace of any movement or any feeling about it, swap yourself over with that imaginary person and stay there for a few seconds, as if you're really there. Then come straight back out of it and notice that the imaginary person is nowhere to be seen and the event is just waiting for you to drop back into later (but by then you'll be the New You).

The procedure

The procedure is presented in mostly outline form, since it's similar to the one you're becoming ever more used to by now, and definitely works best if you record it and listen with your eyes closed.

1. Focus on the Assessment Event and *feel* the PAL.

2. Stop and Stare the event so that nothing is moving.

3. Now into the Virtual Reality section:
   - Focus on the Stop and Stare image.
   - Immediately block it with the New You image in the same event, looking for all the world as though you [*insert chosen phrase*].
   - Focus on where you feel the New You in your body.
   - See thousands of flashes of neural pathways lighting up all over the brain.
   - Now dive straight into the waiting Ideal Future as the New You.
   - The Ideal Future immediately becomes active and you can zoom in to actually become the New You and make this part last slightly longer each time you get to this step.

4. Repeat step 3 five more times, quickly.

5. Drift down into the reptilian complex for the Super Unwind – Part Two (see page 22) for just a few minutes.

6.   After returning to full awareness, bring the Assessment Event to mind; check the PAL and repeat the procedure if necessary.

Text to record

1.   'Focus on the assessment event, make it vivid in your mind and really *feel* the PAL.' (5-second pause)

2.   'Now Stop and Stare that event to stop it dead, so nothing is moving.' (2-second pause)

3.   'Now focus on that stopped image.'

4.   (Fast and urgent from now on) 'Immediately block it with the New You image in the same event, and looking for all the world as though you [*insert chosen phrase*].'

5.   'Focus on where you feel the New You in your body as thousands of flashes of neural pathways light up all over your brain.'

6.   'Now dive straight into that waiting Ideal Future as the New You and the flashes of neural pathways increase as the Ideal Future becomes active.'

7.   'Now zoom right in to actually become that New You and savour every moment of being part of that scene.'

Repeat steps 3–7 five more times, speaking as quickly as you can but pausing on step 7; for 1 second the first time, 2 seconds the second time, 3 on the third and so on. Then continue with:

8.   'Now drift down into the reptilian complex for the Super Unwind – Part Two.'

That's the end of the recording and after returning to full awareness open your eyes, bring the Assessment Event to mind and check the PAL again. It should now be considerably reduced, though you can repeat the procedure to lower it further if you want to. It might be that you have now already sorted out your main problem, but read on because there's a lot more interesting stuff to come. And if, for any reason at all, this chapter didn't do it for you, then the more advanced work in Chapters 15 and 16 should get you on top form.

Chapter 8

All About Anxiety

Before we can set about relieving anxiety (as far as it is possible to do so) we need to consider whether it is just anxiety or whether there's a stress situation that needs to be resolved first. Stress and anxiety are often used interchangeably, though the modern approach is that the one – anxiety – is caused by the other – stress. But that's not the whole picture. Anxiety can and does arise without any genuine stressor being present, requiring a different process from that which deals with stressors.

So, the first thing to do is to examine half-a-dozen common stress triggers and how we might deal with any of them. They will generally not need any BWRT technique to be applied – just a decision to be made. Here's the list:

1. **Being pulled in two directions at once:** Not knowing what course of action to take and therefore doing nothing at all, or running around like a chicken with its head cut off. The anxiety is about making the wrong decision by somebody else's, or even everybody else's, standards.

   Strategy: There is no response that will keep everybody happy, so all you can do in these circumstances is what works best for you. Use both parts of the Super Unwind (see pages 21–23) to offset any dissent.

2. **Workload problems:** Not having enough time to do everything that is required or demanded of you and therefore working under pressure. This is usually based on the fear of suffering some consequence as a result of error or ineffectiveness.

   Strategy: The only thing that can help here is to keep calm and carry on, doing the best you can. If it all blows up at some point, then that's an opportunity for discussion. Again, the Super Unwind technique will help greatly.

3. **Excessively high expectations of self:** This is probably the worst, most common and most unnecessary stress trigger. Usually, everybody else is happy with what you do – but you don't believe that, so drive yourself even harder. The situation is continuous and tends to affect a large part of life including career and relationships.

   Strategy: Complete the material in Chapter 7, even if you feel you do not have low self-worth. It's just the same problem with another face.

4. **Demands too great for your skill:** This feels like a threat to your integrity, sometimes with an accompanying fear of letting someone down or being seen to be stupid or worthless.

   Strategy: If you're certain that your skills really are lacking, search out that which you need to know. Otherwise complete the material in Chapter 7, which works well for lack of self-confidence.

5. **Guilt:** The perception that the game may soon be up is the worst part of this one. Often the guilt is unwarranted, or out of proportion to the event or situation, and might give rise to feelings of doom, mild paranoia, persecution and similar.

   Strategy: Working with a guilty secret (see Chapter 5) is the best way forward – though where the guilt is warranted, owning up might be the only solution. That will relieve the stress but might create other problems, of course; your choice.

6. **An uncomfortable situation:** It's when you are unable to make any sort of worthwhile change that this one really makes itself felt. The ancient fight or flight response will be triggered and it's when you are not able to take any action that the resultant stress starts to really bite.

   Strategy: Sit it out, using both parts of the Super Unwind (see pages 21–23) to offset the stress.

Of course, there are many other possibilities. But those listed are common and even if none of them are relevant to you, it's likely they will lead you into a recognition of anything that is presently affecting you. The important thing about all stressors is that until they're resolved in some way, or elim-inated, they don't magically stop stressing you when, or if, you get used to them – they just do it in the background instead. So seek a solution or take the advice for (6): just sit it out, using the Super Unwind to make life easier.

Anxiety

Anxiety comes in many forms and tends to affect people in different ways, depending on their lifestyle, family background and upbringing, personality type, age, gender and even culture (if that differs from their current situation). It's not just how it makes you feel that's the problem, but the effects on your health – especially if it's the result of long-term stress. It can be helpful to understand exactly why it does have such an effect on health because this can add impetus to your attempts to sort it out once and for all. So we're going to take a little diversion from the world of psychology, just briefly, into the domain of physiology: the way the physical body responds to stress and anxiety, and how it repairs itself when all is working exactly as it should be. Welcome to the world of DNA, telomeres and telomerase.

Every strand of DNA in your body cells has an *end cap* called a telomere – a bit like the plastic or metal ends on a shoelace. The telomere is made up of thousands of copies of the end part of the DNA strand and just one copy gets lost every time the cell divides. But the pattern is repeated, so that loss is not that important at first. Eventually, though, the last copy of that part of the DNA strand disappears when the telomere is totally depleted, and that cell then dies. The more cells we lose, the more our health deteriorates and the less quickly we can recover from illness. Enough cells are lost eventually that life simply cannot be sustained any longer – but don't despair just yet because the body is, for the most part, a self-repairing machine.

Telomerase is an enzyme that has the important task of replenishing the lost part of the telomere. Most of it is in the stem cells found in many parts of the body, such as the brain, bone marrow, blood, blood vessels, skeletal muscles, skin and the liver. They are activated by disease or injury to replenish damaged cells and some even have the ability for total regeneration, as in the liver and fingertips. This all sounds like good news, but there's a problem. And now we're back to psychology: psychological stress – and subsequently raised cortisol levels – depletes the supply of telomerase. So the good news is that your body is a self-repairing machine for most of your life; the bad news is that stress and anxiety mess about with that repair mechanism. The more effectively you can manage stress and subsequent anxiety, therefore, the healthier and long-lived you're likely to be. We're not talking here about only major illness (contrary to popular belief, scientific evidence indicates that stress and anxiety are not a major cause of cancer) but of all sorts of ailments that your immune system is designed to defend you from: the minor colds and stomach upsets, the rashes that appear out of nowhere, the sudden onset of allergies you've never experienced before, and more serious conditions like autoimmune disorders where your body starts to attack itself. You've probably already read about that in Chapter 5.

There are a huge number of methods available to relieve anxiety and not one of them will work for everybody. Apart from medication and the hundreds of self-help books and courses, they include hypnotherapy, hypnoanalysis, psychotherapy, meditation, eye movement desensitisation and reprocessing (EMDR), emotional freedom technique (EFT), Thought Field Therapy (TFT), cognitive behavioural therapy (CBT) and many more. They all work, to one degree or another, but many have found that there are none as consistently effective in the hands of the professional therapist as BWRT.[1] Although there is not a therapy in the world that will always work for absolutely everybody, BWRT comes close – and it can certainly never make things worse, which is a risk with some other methods. The version of BWRT you're learning here is obviously not as powerful as the pro version – but it comes a very close second.

The faces of anxiety

In this chapter we're going to have a brief look at the main styles that anxiety can take, as well as some general information that is relevant to all of them; some of the specific forms are dealt with in separate chapters later. It is a fact that all anxiety is a diluted version of fear, as you read in Chapter 3, and one of the reasons that BWRT is so effective is that it seeks to get directly to the triggers of that fear at the very source – the reptilian complex. The Stop and Stare process is a major part of that, of course, so do practise that until you can do it easily whenever you want to; when you get it right there will be nothing else at all in your mind except the stationary scene you're staring at.

The major recognised forms of anxiety that are suitable for work with BWRT are:

- **Specific event anxiety:** Associated with things like exams and tests, hospitalisation, weddings, illness and other one-off situations.

---

1 See https://www.bwrt.org/ and https://bwrtsa.co.za/.

- **Generalised anxiety disorder (GAD):** Many normal everyday situations trigger a response.

- **Free-floating anxiety:** The state of anxiety is present a lot of the time – maybe almost all the time – but with no specific connection to any event or situation.

- **Simple phobia:** A profound irrational fear about situations and concepts where there is no threat to life, such as fear of wasps, mice, spiders, etc.

- **Complex phobia:** Not a true phobia as such, but a partly rational profound fear about situations and concepts where the risk to life is greatly exaggerated; examples being aeroplane flights, driving in heavy traffic, escalators, heights, etc.

- **FTSD (future traumatic stress disorder):** Fear of some future event or circumstance which is exaggerated in its likelihood; health anxiety (hypochondria), for example – but other possibilities can trigger it, such as being falsely accused of something, or bankruptcy, for instance. This one is not really suitable for self-help, so is not covered in this book.

Dealing with it

There is no universal fix that will work to alleviate all forms of anxiety, but there is much you can do that will weaken its grip. The first (and probably the least popular) is physical exercise, along with a healthy diet. These concepts, which come under the general heading of *lifestyle*, are not part of this book – that is a vast subject about physiology and this book is about psychology. Suffice to say that exercise often increases the body's production of endorphins (the body's feel-good hormone), reduces stress and inflammation, and can result in better physical health and potentially a longer life. So, if you're something of an anxious couch potato, you might consider investing in a pair of running shoes. Well, okay then – a trial gym membership.

But if you're not into physical exertion – with the accompanying sweating, huffing and puffing – there are other things you can do that will help to diminish any of the above forms of anxiety. Although the techniques mentioned in this chapter are really just an offset and probably not as effective as some of the material later in the book, they are still worth learning and being familiar with. The first one is something you've already learned: the Super Unwind from Chapter 2 (see pages 21–23). You can use either just

Part One or, for the deluxe self-treatment, give yourself a 30-minute break and do Parts One and Two. The relief might only be temporary if there's something in your life that is driving the anxiety, but it cannot fail to leave you feeling better than you were to begin with.

The second technique is not BWRT, nor is it original, but it's included here because it's almost always effective – it's also easy to use because you don't have to learn to do anything you don't already do:

Belly breathing

This can create a profound state of relaxation within which anxiety cannot function. Here's how to do it:

1. Settle yourself quietly in an armchair (you can do this exercise lying down, though sitting is slightly better).

2. Now place your hands, one loosely over the other, on your solar plexus (just above your navel) and allow your face to become completely and utterly expressionless so that anybody looking at you would not have the first idea what you're thinking. You might have to work at the expressionless face for a moment or two, thinking especially about your forehead and the muscles around your eyes and mouth. Keeping your face as expressionless as possible is a message to the reptilian complex that there's nothing going on that needs any attention – after all, if there were, your face would be reacting in some way.

3. Now breathe slowly and steadily without trying to count the seconds in and out, as you might have read elsewhere – it's not necessary for this exercise. As you breathe in each time, you should feel it through your hands as your stomach rises and falls gently with each breath.

If you don't feel your hands moving, you are probably breathing by using the chest muscles – often the case in the anxiety sufferer – which has been shown to often increase anxiety levels.[2] This is not a surprise because the only times it would be normal to breathe via the chest would be during physical exertion or as a response to genuine fear triggering the fight or flight response.

---

2   S. Ankrom, 8 Deep Breathing Exercises to Reduce Anxiety, *verywellmind* [blog] (20 March 2021). Available at: https://www.verywellmind.com/abdominal-breathing-2584115.

So it's entirely probable that chest breathing creates feelings of anxiety because the reptilian complex perceives that (a) you are involved in physical exertion and therefore increases adrenaline that, undischarged, can result in anxiety surges; or (b) danger is present and reacts with a fear/anxiety response.

Learning to breathe from the stomach is sometimes quite difficult when you have the habit of breathing through the chest; it can even feel as if the whole idea is incorrect or in some way awkward. Practice makes perfect, however, and it will eventually become normal for you to breathe that way all the time, unless you truly do need more oxygen in your bloodstream for some reason – but then that wouldn't trigger anxiety.

The third technique is extremely fast and effective but is not as relaxing, nor probably as long-lasting as the first two, and only of use where there's a specific situation that you've encountered once before which is acting as a trigger.

- Bring the event to mind and make it vivid.
- Take a very fast breath and hold it while you Stop and Stare the scene.
- Imagine it immediately scrolls off and away in whatever direction feels right to you.

The techniques shown here will help you in the short term, but read on to discover more permanent solutions for the types of anxiety listed earlier.

Chapter 9

Fixing Generalised Anxiety Disorder

Generalised anxiety disorder (GAD) is often misunderstood. It is not a serious personality disorder, an indicator of some kind of underlying personal weakness or the result of playing too many violent video games. Neither is it associated with low intelligence, lack of moral fibre or poor psychological resilience. It is, in fact, nothing more than the result of the brain's safety and survival systems firing up and doing exactly what they are supposed to be doing – seeking to keep the sufferer out of harm's way. Before we go any further we'll look first at what GAD is – then at a few situations that often get classed as such, when they are actually something quite different.

From a health professional's point of view, GAD is a chronic condition lasting for six months or more, where an individual worries about all manner of things that are usually not the cause of anxiety (or excessive anxiety, anyway) for most people. It can include fretting about health, as well as everyday events like answering the telephone, interacting with others, driving, getting ready for work, preparing meals and more – but it certainly won't be just one of those things. It will also fire up in less usual situations: during a thunder storm, for example; the sea (even just the sight of rolling waves); when people are drunk, or arguing and shouting; going into new situations – in other words, a whole lot of apparently unconnected concepts can trigger the response. Some feel it as a distinct fear of being in some way out of control of life and therefore at risk; others just have the heebie-jeebies over almost everything and are not even able to remember the last time they didn't feel anxious about something. What marks it out as GAD is that the anxiety is irrational and a lot of the time totally unwarranted, and yet it is apparent that the reptilian complex perceives the presence of threat.

Some seek to control it with medication; others with alcohol, drugs, sex, meditation, or a variety of over-the-counter herbs and potions that may or may not bring relief. But to get a lasting result it's necessary to defuse the underlying driver – and, fortunately, with BWRT we can do that without having to find out what it is.

Later you'll learn a procedure that, although *consumer BWRT*, runs in a manner that is quite similar to the way a professional practitioner would approach it. First, though, we'll have a look at a few other situations that are (from time to time) erroneously labelled as GAD. The main one of these is called free-floating anxiety and it's easy to see how the error occurs. The sufferer will state that everything makes them anxious, but there is a major difference between that and GAD. In the latter, there are always a number of things the individual knows do not make them anxious, whereas in the free-floating version the feeling of threat seems to be present at some level or another all the time, even though they may have no idea at all what that threat might be. There's more, but that will be discussed in detail in the next chapter (which is dedicated to that particular issue).

Other situations sometimes wrongly attributed as GAD include: constant fears about the future, worrying all the time about a single but unlikely possibility, continual anxiety about issues such as relationships or career. While these can be debilitating to normal life, they are focused rather than generalised and can usually be helped greatly by following exactly the standard procedure given in Chapter 3. That will, in fact, work effectively with almost any one-off or single focus situation, though you might sometimes need a bit of thought to see how to get the best out of it.

The origins

Most people suffering from GAD have been sensitised (even if that is not immediately obvious) and that is likely to have originated in one of two ways:

■ Constant displays of anxiety about all manner of things by one or both parents, conveying the impression that threat lurks undetected around every corner; it is entirely possible that they were primed by their own families, giving rise to the belief that it runs in the family, which can negatively affect any trust in the idea that it is possible to be free from it.

- A chain of disconnected events ranging from the minor to the disastrous, where there is a distinct sensation of one thing after another happening for an extended period of time; this is accompanied by an increasing sense of depression and resigned acceptance, along with a watchfulness for what will transpire next – and we always find that which we seek.

It might be the case that you feel neither situation applies to you, or that, if either of them do, they are not the reason for your own GAD – and you could be right. But if one or both of those situations does feel familiar, it's important to be aware that there were many times when an anxiety did not turn out to be well founded (rather than fixate on the times it did). That's easier said than done, unfortunately, since we are all hard-wired to be more aware of threat than safety. When the idea is gained that normal everyday life and events carry potential threats to safety, then GAD can be generated – and once it's there it tends to be self-supporting; every event that turns out as feared confirms that the anxiety was entirely justified. And yet, at some level, many people are aware that this idea is false, or they would not be trying to sort it out.

It's unusual for anybody to be able to state exactly why they are anxious about their particular triggers. They might be anxious about telephone calls in case they hear bad news, anxious about social events in case somebody falls ill, anxious about storms in case they get struck by lightning, anxious about travelling in case there's an accident, and so on. This is exactly why it's called *generalised* anxiety disorder, of course. Underneath it all there will be an invisible personal fear that unifies all triggers, though discovering what it is in order to work with it can prove to be a lengthy task. Some professional therapists rely on analytical or investigative techniques to track down the underlying cause. This can work really well but it has a few snags: (1) it's far from a fast therapy, as a rule; (2) it can be uncomfortable for the client who has to trawl through the early years of their life; (3) there are often multiple causes and finding one is no guarantee of success. Other practitioners rely on cognitive behavioural therapy (CBT), part of which involves the sufferer making notes of their thoughts around their anxiety every day. This also works – until the process is abandoned for being tedious. Others rely on counselling, the main downside of which is that it often tends towards a lengthy series of sessions.

Fortunately, we don't need to do that with BWRT. We don't have to find the original cause of the triggers to be successful and it's not necessary for anybody to make reams of notes or attend therapy on a weekly basis for months or years. Usually, in fact, we just need to rapidly defuse/deactivate the worst few of the triggers and the rest fade into insignificance. And there's a very sound reason for this. Completely defusing the worst triggers in a short time sends a message to the reptilian complex that the alarm for each was false and therefore that invisible personal fear is irrelevant or unfounded.

The method

As mentioned earlier, the work method we're going to use here is very similar – as far as the preparation is concerned – to that employed by a professional BWRT practitioner. The first thing to do is bring to mind a bad day; a day when the anxiety was as high as it can get. It doesn't matter if it was yesterday, last week or a few years ago and the only important thing is that you need to be able to remember how it felt, even if you can't find that feeling now. Give the PAL score and if that was only, say, 8 (or lower), then you must be comparing it with something else that was a 9 or a 10 and that's the one you want to find – the 10, ideally. In your mind, go through that day and write down each thing that went wrong or that you were worried about. There's no need to rush the task – make sure you've really captured the essence of it all.

Now you're going to add to the list anything and everything that you know can make you feel anywhere between slightly uncomfortable and on the verge of full-blown panic – oh, all right then, over the verge and into hysterics if you can find it. The important thing is not to leave anything out, whether or not it was in your bad day. It's often difficult to recall the triggers when you're asked to, so here's a list to get you started – some of them might remind you of something that's not mentioned and that's good. Add it to your list.

Social situations	Clothes shopping	Gales/storms
Telephone calls	Eating in restaurants	Illness
Talking to strangers	Drunken people	Changing rooms
Heavy traffic	Shouting/arguing	Eye contact
The sea	Thunder and lightning	Noisy crowds
Driving	Horses	Dogs
Cats	Children	Germs

Handwriting	Talking about money	Talking about sex
Signing documents	Asking favours	Making a complaint
Saying 'no'	Technology	Doctors/consultants

When you have compiled your list, you might find yourself feeling anxious or despondent but that's quite normal and the first part of the work is to allow you to be more at ease with the next stage. Do nothing more with the list on the day you create it, except to put it somewhere out of sight, while knowing in your mind you'll come back to it as soon as you're ready – and when you're ready will be soon enough. First, remind yourself that these things didn't just pop up in your life; you've chosen them to work with. Second, they are not the triggers themselves but simply the labels that allow you to identify them. Third, they are only written down on your paper because you decided to write them there, which means you were in total control throughout. Let those three points stay in your mind for a few moments and notice that any discomfort begins to fade quite quickly.

Now do both parts of the Super Unwind (see pages 21–23) and leave it at that until you decide it's time, whether that's the same day or a month or more later. It's best to avoid reading anything else in this book until you've completed this section (unless you're reading it just because it's there, of course, and don't actually suffer with GAD).

It's time

Okay, here you are and you're feeling ready to get working on those triggers, which is a positive indicator in itself that you'll get a good result from the procedure. As you look over your list, you'll notice that some feel worse than others, which means that some feel less arousing than others – those are the ones we're interested in to begin with. So now rewrite the list starting with the one that causes the least problems; the one that you might only have put in there because it occasionally causes a mild issue. Follow that with the next least *triggery* one, which might be the same or might carry just a little more *triggeriness*, and then continue like that until you have everything listed, with the strongest ones appearing last. Those are the ones we'll be working with first, but there's still one more task to complete before we start.

Take the bottom four from your list (the highest scored), at least one of which should be a 10 on the PAL scale, and decide which one you would choose first if it was the only one you were going to work on – it won't necessarily be the highest scored, but perhaps the one you have to deal with most often. For instance, if *driving in traffic* was scored as an 8 and *thunder and lightning* was rated as a 10, you might choose to work with driving first since you experience it more often. So grade those four highest-scored in the order you want to work with them. You'll be using the same procedure for each trigger, though only working on three on any one occasion – trying to work on all four at once might work but it's likely that, by the time you got to that fourth one, your concentration would be less intense than ideal for the task. There is a very good reason for choosing four in the first place though, as you'll shortly see. The procedure you learned in Chapter 3 is ideal for this exercise, so choose your key words from the two lists, repeated here:

Set 1	Set 2
enthusiastic	cautious
relaxed	careful
energised	aware
relieved	watchful
happy	accepting
calm	sensible
confident	tolerant
at ease	

Remember that if there is no genuine reason for fear, then choose both words from set 1. Otherwise choose one from each set and, whatever is chosen, link them together with *and* or *but* to make sense. As before, the phrase embodies how you want the New You to respond or feel when encountering the trigger. Now think of a familiar situation where you feel exactly like that New You phrase, notice exactly where you feel it in your body and create an image in your mind or thoughts. Next, of course, you need to create the Ideal Future just as you've done before, leaving the scene ready for you to drop into. All that remains now is to decide which Stop method would be the best one to use; if the trigger relates to something you've seen but were not directly involved with in any way, use the Glass Encapsulation method in Chapter 3 (see page 29), but if it's something you've experienced as being a part of, or if it's just an idea that worries you (you'll need to create a mind picture of that) then you'll use the Stop and Stare technique (refer to page 28).

The procedure

Just an outline is given here, rather than a full description, since it has been covered a few times now. There are two methods here: one for when you're using the Stop and Stare process, the other for the Glass Encapsulation. Do be sure to read to the end of this chapter, though, before starting any work.

Stop and Stare

1. Bring the first trigger to mind and make it feel as bad as you can handle.

2. Stop and Stare the scene, then close your eyes.

3. Now for the Virtual Reality section:
   - Focus on the stopped image.
   - Immediately block it with the New You image.
   - Focus on the feeling of the New You in your body.
   - See thousands of flashes of neural pathways lighting up in the brain, going from front to back and side to side.
   - Dive into the waiting Ideal Future as the New You.
   - Zoom in to actually become the New You as the Ideal Future becomes active.

4. Repeat step 3 five more times, quickly.

5. Drift down into the reptilian complex and into the Super Unwind – Part Two (see page 22).

6. Once back up to full awareness, check the PAL of the trigger again and repeat the procedure once or twice if the PAL is higher than 3 – this often won't be necessary.

Text to record

1. 'Think of [*insert trigger here*] and make it as uncomfortable as you can bear.' (5-second pause)

2. 'Stop and Stare to completely freeze it in time.' (2-second pause)

3. 'Now focus on that stopped image and immediately block it with the New You image.'

4.   (Fast and urgent from now on) 'Focus really vividly on that New You feeling in your body as thousands of flashes of neural pathways light up in your brain, going from front to back and side to side.'

5.   'And while that's happening dive into that Ideal Future as the New You.'

6.   'And now zoom right in to actually become that New You as that Ideal Future becomes active just like real life.'

Repeat steps 3–6, going as fast as you can. As you've probably read before, mistakes or stumbles are not important so just keep going if anything like that happens. Continue with:

7.   'Drift down into the reptilian complex and into the Super Unwind – Part Two.'

That's the end of the recording for the Stop and Stare procedure for GAD – and when you've returned to full awareness, open your eyes and check the PAL. If it's higher than 3, repeat the procedure (though this often won't be necessary). If you are certain you will not be using the Glass Encapsulation, continue to the next heading entitled *Important Information* (see page 92).

Glass Encapsulation

In situations where you were not directly involved, this method works best. We work in an entirely different way here. You still need to create the New You image as you did in the previous procedure (you don't need to be involved in any situation for this one) but we won't be using the Ideal Future here, nor the Super Unwind afterwards.

1.   Bring the trigger image to mind and make it as bad as you can handle.

2.   As you stare at the scene, it gradually becomes encased in a kind of glassy substance so that everything is stopped.

3.   Shrink the scene down to a cube-shaped block, small enough for you to pick up and move (as in Chapter 3).

4.   See yourself as if from the outside, picking up the cube and putting it on a storage shelf in a strongroom.

5.   Let go of it to instantly become the New You and see the cube start to fade, or disintegrate a little.

6.   Stare at the cube until it fades or disintegrates a little more.

7. Focus on the feeling of the New You in your body.

8. Count to five at 1-second intervals – do not use a timer or watch.

9. With each count see thousands of flashes of neural pathways lighting up in the brain.

10. Focus on the feeling of the New You in your body again, then zoom in to actually become that New You for just a moment.

11. Repeat steps 6–10 five more times.

12. Leave the strongroom and slam the door shut hard, hearing it clang.

13. Check the PAL – if there's no change, abandon the trigger on this occasion and move on to one of the others. If it's lower, but still higher than 3, repeat steps 6–12 until no further reduction can be felt.

Text to record

1. 'Think of [*insert trigger here*] and make it as bad as you can bear.' (5-second pause)

2. 'As you stare at the scene it quickly gets encased in some sort of glassy substance so that everything stops dead.' (5-second pause)

3. (Quickly, urgently) 'Now imagine the scene shrinking down to a cube-shaped block small enough for you to pick up and carry.'

4. (Not too fast from now on) 'See yourself as the old self, picking that cube up and putting it on a storage shelf in a strongroom and as you let go of it you instantly become the New You and the cube starts to fade or disintegrate.'

5. 'Now stare at the cube until it starts to fade or disintegrate a bit more.'

6. 'Focus strongly on the feeling of the New You in your body and count from one to five with thousands of flashes of neural pathways happening on every count.' (5-second pause)

7. 'Now focus really strongly on the feeling of the New You in your body again, then zoom in to actually become that New You for a moment.'

Repeat steps 5–7 five more times. Notice that this procedure doesn't use high speed in the approach – it would not be possible to imagine the events clearly enough to get the best result if going too fast. Continue with:

8.   'Now leave the strongroom and slam the door hard shut and hear it
       clang.'

That's the end of the recording. After a few seconds open your eyes and
check the PAL – if there's no change, abandon the trigger on this occasion
and move on to one of the others. If it's lower, but still higher than 3, repeat
steps 5–7 until no further reduction can be felt.

Important Information

Whichever procedure you use, you might not get the PAL down to below 3
(though it's excellent if you do) since the reptilian complex must now
reorganise all the other triggers, which will be in some way related. If the
PAL remains higher than 3 after a third attempt, it's time to quit for that
session; if it's 3 or lower, though, repeat immediately with the second and
third triggers, as you feel able. After a time, you will probably feel your
concentration fading; that's the time to stop until the next day.

One of two situations will then be present:

1.   You still have some, or all, the triggers to work through. If necessary,
       add the next one or two from your list to arrive at four triggers again
       and work as before.
2.   You have completed the first three triggers, so you can now check
       the PAL of the fourth – if this is now at 3 or lower, you can move on
       to the Closure Test below. This is why we always work with four
       triggers. If it's still higher than 3, add the next three from the list (to
       again arrive at four triggers) and repeat the process.

Closure Test

Avoid being tempted to try this until checking the fourth trigger gives a PAL
of 3 or less without carrying out any work on it – this automatic lowering of
the PAL indicates that your reptilian complex has already done a lot of work
in the background and it's time to test it. The test itself is very simple: go
back to that original *bad day* memory – the one that was a 9 or 10 on the
PAL scale – and explore it thoroughly. Be sure to immerse into the memory
as much as you possibly can to get the PAL as it is now – it should definitely
be lower and might well be down to a 3 or less, which would indicate that
the overall levels of GAD have been reduced to manageable levels. At this
point you can choose whether to wait and see how life feels now or continue work with the remaining triggers – but don't be surprised if they all

have a lower score than they did at first. Where the *bad day* PAL is still higher than 3, rescore the remaining items on your list; if none of them are at the new PAL of the bad day, search to see what triggers you've missed out. That done, repeat the complete procedure as necessary.

GAD is seldom fully resolved in only one or two sessions, so ignore any despondency if you have to repeat the procedures several times. Just enjoy the bits that have improved while you work on the rest.

Next, one of the most complicated issues to sort out – but with BWRT you can do it.

Chapter 10

Fixing Free-Floating Anxiety Disorder

Before starting on the details of this chapter, there is one concept that is even more important here than in other issues you might work at: if you enjoy even the tiniest benefit from whatever ails you, change is unlikely to stick – even if it occurs to start with.

We touched upon this in Chapter 6, but it's so important it bears repeating. Where you enjoy a benefit of some sort (usually attention, being thought of as a poor little devil, or getting out of doing something) then you have a choice to make: (a) decide to stay as you are and continue to get the attention from those who may view you as somebody who is inadequate at coping with everyday life, or (b) decide to fix the whole thing and get even more attention by being an inspiration to those others. It's a well-known concept in professional circles (where it's known as having an agenda or a gain) and often results in the therapy failing, leaving the individual with the problem feeling oddly triumphant. If you recognise this process in yourself, there is little point in continuing with the material in this book unless you can honestly decide that enough is enough, and forgo the benefit so that you can be free to find the best version of you that could ever exist.

Before looking at the intricacies of free-floating anxiety, an important piece of advice is in order:

If you've not been tested for medical causes of anxiety – particularly for issues with your thyroid gland and deficiency in vitamins D3 and B12 – then it would be a good idea to request these from your GP, along with a check for other possible causes (such as autoimmune disorders) before continuing with the material here.

Free-floating anxiety revealed

Okay, you're still here – so let's have a close look at what can be a puzzling condition. One of the problems is that there is no specific symptom pattern associated with any object or situation and the only way you might know you have it is because you feel anxious almost all the time, even though you can't really say why. Most of the time it's not just an awareness of anxiety, as such, but sensations in the gut, arms, legs, head or any other part of the body.

Those physical sensations might be a churning sensation, butterflies, restless legs, palpitations, sudden physical weakness, a panic attack (which might last only seconds, or for an hour or more), visual disturbances, nausea, dizziness, foreboding, feelings of doom, bowel disturbance and countless other sensations. Because this type of anxiety is a master of disguise, it can even take the form of a belief that some sinister unknown illness is present, resulting in many visits to the GP or medical consultant, copious tests, and the only diagnosis being made is that the patient is either a hypochondriac or suffering from anxiety. The belief and sense of threat is so real, however, that this diagnosis is usually hotly denied.

Where it is recognised as anxiety, though, it might have been present for as long as the individual can remember, or suddenly be fired up by the triggering of an underlying cause that may have lain dormant in the psyche for many years. Such late onset anxiety occurs when some relatively minor event passes almost unnoticed but echoes something from the distant past, and the reptilian complex (that never forgets anything without it being made safe) goes into full alert status. The problem is that the trigger was only a reminder and now almost everything is searched in case a threat is present – and to the conscious mind that search feels like anxiety itself.

It's entirely possible that you are convinced there is some traumatic event at the root of it all, as many who suffer this condition are. This is possible if the event was during your early childhood years and has been consciously forgotten but, though that sort of thing does happen, it's completely beyond the scope of this book to investigate for such an event. And if there's a traumatic happening that you can remember, it's unlikely to be the cause of this type of anxiety (though it would certainly cause some of the other issues discussed in this book).

One of the most likely causes is a major change or a series of big changes during your younger years that precipitated fear, unhappiness or other events perceived as distressing in some way. If you are aware of events such as these, it's feasible that they are at the core of your anxiety – even if that doesn't feel right, because not feeling right is a response the reptilian complex uses to keep you from investigating and feeling the same distress all over again.

Important: if these events are just a memory, and carry no immediate feeling or response, it is perfectly safe to continue with the work in this chapter without further exploration of them. If, however, you have a strong urge to explore the situation, you are strongly advised to do so only with the help of a registered BWRT practitioner.

We're talking here about traumatic change that produced a major upheaval in life, not a simple change such as from one school to another. Examples are:

- Parents divorcing acrimoniously and fighting over custody.
- The introduction, without warning, of a new sibling (perhaps via adoption or as a result of a new relationship) resulting in loss of status or personal space.
- Sudden drastically reduced living standards for any reason.
- Illness or death of one or both parents, especially in traumatic circumstances.
- Unexpected relocation to a completely new environment.
- Accidental discovery of being adopted.
- Discovery of previous criminality or scandal in one or both parents' lives.

There are many other possibilities, of course, but they always have the same effect of striking at the very core of an individual's existence – although not necessarily causing the same amount of damage in all individuals. And now we're into one of the most interesting and, at the same time, perplexing concepts as far as anxiety is concerned: personality. This governs how an individual responds to anxiety triggers so that something one person finds acutely distressing is of less consequence to another, and is possibly even exciting instead. We're not going into a full exploration of personality here but we will look at how to establish the sort of event that might be the source of any triggers you might have. For our purposes here, we can reference a system which is easy to understand and has fascinated many thousands of individuals, including therapists of all persuasions, since 2000 when it was first introduced in the book, *Warriors, Settlers & Nomads*.[1]

We're not using any personality test here; all that is necessary is to identify yourself via brief descriptions, which will allow the procedure later to be tailored to fit your personality more accurately. This enables us to work more successfully with this type of anxiety than would otherwise be possible. The professional version of BWRT uses a system that is too complicated to be incorporated into a self-help book; what you'll be using is BWRT-like, though, and although not truly comparable to the professional version, is still effective – though might need a brief top-up session from time to time.

There are four brief descriptions to choose from and, although you will discover you have something of each in your personality make-up, it is almost always the case that one type is clearly dominant. In each case there are two negative attributes listed and an honest appraisal will often reveal the real you.

Warrior

This is a no-nonsense person who is practical and down-to-earth, being unimpressed by outlandish claims or airy-fairy nonsense. They are a good planner and organiser, like to be always in control and can easily be irritated by the mistakes of others.

Positives: Forthright, direct, tenacious, organised, sensible, observant.

Negatives: Critical, hate being seen to be in the wrong.

Settler

The Settlers are the nice people in the world; trusting, helpful to others and will usually lend a helping hand where it is needed. They are highly intuitive and adaptable, are very community-minded and have difficulty in refusing requests of any sort.

Positives: Kind, sympathetic, friendly, supportive, agreeable, nurturing.

---

1   T. Watts, *Warriors, Settlers & Nomads: Discovering Who We Are and What We Can Be* (Carmarthen: Crown House Publishing, 2000).

Negatives: Can sulk longer than most, easily upset.

Nomad

The Nomads will usually be either extremely elegant or extremely scruffy and maybe both at different times. They are ideas people and sometimes have trouble staying with a plan long enough to complete it. They love to tell stories, which are often exaggerated.

Positives: Enthusiastic, energetic, excitable, dramatic, inventive, charismatic.

Negatives: Can be shallow, lie easily.

Combination

As the title suggests, the Combination personality exhibits something of each type so that it is difficult to define them from any of the descriptions above. Some seem to not have much to offer the world; others are power-houses, displaying the best qualities of the other three types.

Positives: Any of those listed above but with a leaning towards Nomad.

Negatives: Any of those listed above but with a strong leaning towards Warrior.

None of the personality types are more or less likely to suffer free-floating anxiety (or any other problem, for that matter) than the others, but the reactions vary and this is why we adapt the procedure for each one. The following lists the likely responses to anxiety and may help to confirm your recognition of your category:

- **Warrior:** Will often be irritated and irritable as a result of anxiety and will usually deny, or try to deny, that they are anxious at all.
- **Settler:** Will usually try to make the best of it in company but will fear they're letting others down in some way. May blame themselves for being weak.
- **Nomad:** Doesn't often *do* anxiety but when they do, are likely to claim they're sure they have a serious illness ticking away; maybe a brain tumour or cancer.

- ◾ **Combination:** Usually curious/puzzled about the cause of it and may spend hours ruminating about whether they've somehow brought it on themselves.

You might be wondering why we didn't look at personality types for GAD (and some of the other issues); it's all to do with the type of procedure we have to use to resolve the problem. With every other issue in the book there are targets and/or particular ideas to focus on in the repair work, but this is not the case with free-floating anxiety and so we have to use a broad-brush approach, which will be far more effective if we can customise it as much as possible. Later you'll see the plug-in phrase for your type, though you can use one of the others if it seems to fit you better. We'll get to those soon but there's a little bit more work to do first.

Locating centres

To get the best result from this procedure, there are two physical centres in the body to access. The first one you might be able to find immediately; if not, a bit of investigation will find it. It is the centre of anxiety in your body – it'll be a physical place; maybe your stomach, chest, solar plexus, or head, perhaps. If you can immediately identify it, that's good and you can write it down. If not, think of all the places you feel anxiety in the body, even if it's not every time. In addition to the places already mentioned, they might include legs, knees, anus, bowel, genitals, hips, shoulders, neck, arms, eyes, ears, top of the head, forehead – almost anywhere in the physical body. The sensation might be a tingling, buzzing or pressure; a hollow or fizzy feeling; feeling weak, heavy, dizzy, wobbly, breathless, pulsating or throbbing, shaking, trembling, faint, nauseous, among other (less common) possibilities. Of course, nobody has all of them but be sure to list all those you do.

When you've located everything, write the physical locations on a sheet of paper to create a body map: at the top of the paper, in the middle, write the location of the highest point in your body where you feel anxiety; then at the bottom, in the middle, write the location of the lowest point. Next, list anything in-between in about the right place – you could use an outline figure but this sometimes creates anxiety where there wasn't any before. Once you have everything written, write the type of anxiety feeling you get next to the relevant part of the body map. Don't worry if it's the same everywhere or different in some places (or every place) because whatever your experience, that's exactly what needs to be shown. Study your diagram for a few minutes – only a few minutes – and see if, without trying, you gradually become aware of the centre of anxiety. If you find it, that's good; if you don't, it just means it's weak (or already beginning to fade) and will more easily be disabled.

Now, as in the GAD process in the last chapter, when you have compiled your list you might find yourself feeling a bit anxious or despondent. This is quite normal and the work so far completed is to allow you to be more at ease with the next stage. Do nothing more with the list on the day you create it, except to put it somewhere out of sight with a decision to come back to it as soon as you're ready – and when you're ready will be soon enough. Now do the complete Super Unwind (see pages 21–23) and leave it at that until you decide it's time – whether that's the same day, or a month or more later. It's best to avoid reading anything else in this book until you've completed this section (unless you're reading it purely out of interest, and don't actually suffer with free-floating anxiety).

It's time

If you've not discovered a physical centre of anxiety in your body, it's not a problem because what you do have is a physical representation on your sheet of paper with the locations and physical sensations listed. There's no need to be able to remember every detail, just the locations. You can prac-tise going to them in your mind a couple of times before we move on to the next step: locating that second physical centre in your body – the centre of calm. You might already have worked out that calmness will be radiating out from this place to every part of your physical self, and maybe even a bit beyond. If you can't immediately feel it, you can choose its position as you prefer – it can be in the same place as the centre of anxiety, or somewhere completely different. It does need to be in a physical location in your body but it's the centre of calm, not necessarily the centre of your body. Before we get to the procedure itself, we have one more task: to create the plug-in personal phrase for your personality type. You'll need to remember it but it's brief, so should present no difficulty, and doesn't have to be word-perfect:

- **Warrior:** 'steady, calm, controlled and focused'
- **Settler:** 'totally at ease with a smile on your face'
- **Nomad:** 'as if you're feeling absolutely fantastic'
- **Combination:** 'as if you've worked it all out and feel good'

The procedure

The Ideal Future isn't used in this procedure, since we're looking at every-day situations and circumstances (rather than improving responses to a single event). Although you might not have realised it yet, a lot of the work has already been done – so in this case the procedure is really just to activate everything. We do still need a New You of course, so create that by seeing yourself in a series of three different situations, like snapshots, where you know you might have felt uneasy but are now looking [*insert your chosen phrase*]. You don't have to believe it or feel it at this stage, just imagine you can see yourself as if from the outside.

Now we're ready to go. You can work with your eyes open if you have a good enough imagination, but it's easy to be distracted that way and the recording is likely to be far superior – the text is given later, as usual.

1. Looking at it from the outside, bring a really bad time to mind – a time when the anxiety was feeling overwhelming. Make it vivid and find as much feeling in it as you are able, or can handle. Get as close to a 10 as possible for the PAL.

2. Stop and Stare the scene so that nothing is moving, not even a single thought.

3. Focus on the stopped image.

4. Immediately block it with the New You image.

5. See those three snapshots in your mind, one after the other in rapid succession.

6. See thousands of flashes of neural pathways lighting up in the brain at the front, back, left, right, whole brain.

7. See the New You looking [*insert chosen phrase*] and make it vivid.

8. Feel the centre of calm radiating outwards past the centre of anxiety and out to all the anxiety points at once; maybe even surrounding your whole body.

9. Zoom in to actually become the New You and feel [*insert chosen phrase*].

10. Repeat steps 3–9 five more times, as quickly as you can.

11. Drift down into the reptilian complex and into the Super Unwind – Part Two (see page 22).

12. Once back up to full awareness, check the PAL of the bad time again and repeat the procedure once or twice if the PAL is higher than 3 – this often won't be necessary.

Text to record

1. 'Bring a really bad time to mind, looking at it as if from the outside. Get the PAL as high as you can and 10 is great.' (5-second pause)

2. 'Stop and Stare it so that nothing is moving; not even a single thought.' (2-second pause)

3. (Urgently) 'Now focus on that stopped image and immediately block it with the New You image.'

4. (Not too fast from here on) 'See those three snapshots of the New You in your mind quickly, one after the other.' (3-second pause)

5. 'See thousands of flashes of neural pathways lighting up in your brain at the front, back, left, right, whole brain.'

6. 'And you can see the New You looking [*insert chosen phrase*] and looking really good.'

7. 'Now feel that centre of calm radiating all around you past the centre of anxiety and out to all the anxiety points at once and maybe even surrounding your whole body.'

8. 'Now zoom right in to actually become the New You and really feel [*insert chosen phrase*] and make it strong.'

Repeat steps 3–8 five more times fairly quickly, with emphasis that feels right to you but at normal speech volume (loudness doesn't actually work that well).

9. 'Drift down into the reptilian complex and into the Super Unwind – Part Two'.

Once back up to full awareness, check the PAL of the bad time again and repeat the procedure once or twice if the PAL is higher than 3 – this often won't be necessary. This procedure can often produce a permanent resolution of anxiety, though it might be necessary to run it in its entirety a few times. Also, you can do this brief mini procedure on a daily basis as needed – just before sleep is perfect. There's no text to record for this one because it's best just doing it in your mind.

The mini procedure

1. Remember the worst event of the day (or a different one if necessary).

2. Stop and Stare the image and immediately drag the New You in front of it.

3. See vivid flashes of neural pathways lighting up in the brain at the front, back, left, right, whole brain.

4. Zoom in to become the New You and feel [*insert chosen phrase*].

5. Repeat steps 1–4 five more times.

Next we're going to have a look at phobias – but they might not be phobias in the way you think of them, as you'll see.

Chapter 11

Phobia – Simple or Complex?

The term *phobia* is often used these days to refer to anything that an individual freaks out about, but that's not the whole picture. There are, in fact, two types of phobia – simple and complex. The latter is not a straightforward phobia in the true sense of the word and needs a different methodology from the simple type to get the best result. We'll have a good look at complex phobias in the next chapter.

Here, though, we're going to work with the simple phobia – but just to avoid any confusion, some clarification is probably a good idea; simple certainly doesn't mean *not very bad*, but indicates that it is centred on a single phobic object. The level of anxiety or abject terror the individual might experience is broadly similar in both types of phobia, but the amount of genuine risk is vastly different:

- **Simple phobia:** A profound and irrational fear – maybe even terror – of something that is unlikely to cause any real or lasting physical harm; examples are spiders, mice, crane flies, earthworms, cats, dogs and speaking in public.

- **Complex phobia:** A profound fear that may be every bit as severe as in the simple phobia and where there is a risk of harm, no matter how slight; examples are flying, driving (especially in heavy or fast traffic), the sea, stairs, escalators, lifts (*elevators* in the USA) and ladders. The fear is sometimes indirect; not associated with the object of the phobia itself but with something else, as you'll see in the next chapter.

There is a grey area in that some species of spider are venomous, many snakes are dangerous and some dogs have been known to kill people, for instance. In cases of this sort (somewhere between the simple and complex) the methodology in Chapter 12 will perhaps be more suitable and effective than that being covered here.

There is another apparent phobic response that tends to be associated mostly with bodily functions such as defaecation, vomiting, urination, eating and sexual function. These are complicated issues and certainly not suitable for self-help, hence there is nothing more about them in this book – but BWRT professionals can and do work with them, usually extremely successfully. They are often caused by an obsessive disorder which is beyond the scope of what is covered here.

The simple phobia

Before we get to the procedure, a bit of psychological preparation will help to diminish any sense of guilt, shame, embarrassment or any other self-deprecating response that is sometimes present in the psyche of the individual with a phobia. As you will read in the next few paragraphs, there is no reason whatsoever to believe or accept that you played any part in the presence of that phobic response. Now, there's quite a lengthy description coming up of the way that a phobia develops; that's because the greater your understanding of it all, the more fantastically effective the procedure will be.

It's important to recognise immediately that you cannot be slightly phobic – if you were, it would just be anxiety. You are either fully phobic about something or you are not. And when you are, your reptilian complex recognises the object as being highly dangerous – possibly even fatal – and so creates an *escape at all costs* response. There is no logic in that part of the brain and once it has triggered the 'run like H---!' signal, fear will instantly flood the psyche and any attempt to rationalise the situation will probably be resisted (or not even noticed). An individual might have a huge panic attack and be hyperventilating and/or sweating and gasping; they might run around blindly, screaming as if Lucifer himself has appeared in front of them; or they might freeze on the spot, faint, burst into tears, or shout an obscenity before vomiting – in other words, an involuntary reaction associated with mortal fear. This is a far cry from the uneasiness associated with what some call slightly phobic.

Not everybody with a phobic response has an extreme reaction, of course, but it will almost always be one that others have difficulty in understanding and may even find irritating – it's hard for others to believe that the response cannot just be controlled. The fact is, though, it can be severe enough that even just discussing the phobic object can produce a reaction, even if usually milder than if it was real at that very moment. Videos can sometimes produce a full reaction because the reptilian complex has recognised a danger pattern and is not sophisticated enough to recognise it's not real. The reason for all this is that logic is a product of the relatively slow modern part of the brain that has existed for around 2.5 million years or less, while the phobic response is linked to the lightning-fast survival instincts that kept our most ancient ancestors alive for hundreds of millions of years. Those who had the most instinctive escape response to, say, sabre-toothed tigers or brown bears were the ones most likely to survive – not those who paused to think or reason. And so their offspring would learn that when they saw a sabre-toothed tiger or a brown bear, the best thing to do was to get out of the way very quickly (unless they themselves were a sabre-toothed tiger or brown bear, of course).

Nature has a wonderful knack of prioritising every tiny element that gives life the best chance of survival, and the best element of them all in that respect is the fear of death. The greater the fear, the better the survival; the better the survival, the more progeny there are to inherit the fear – elegance in nature. There is a school of thought that suggests the fear of death underpins all anxiety and there is much to be said for that argument; it certainly makes sense of some of the extreme reactions that are occasionally exhibited in the phobic response. On occasions, an individual could not scream any louder (or faint any faster), if the grim reaper himself knocked on their door.

Conditioning

There is some evidence that we have an inherited distaste for creepy-crawlies like spiders and cockroaches, perhaps because we associate them with death and decay. This might also be the case for small scurrying creatures like mice. But the abject fear and panic some people have with such things is very far beyond distaste and more likely to be associated with the psychological response of conditioned fear. In psychology, conditioning is described as a behavioural process whereby a response becomes more frequent (or more predictable) in a given environment, as a result of reinforcement. Such conditioning usually comes early in life from the observation of elders. If they run about screaming blue murder because a mouse has popped its head round the door, or a spider that has suddenly appeared in front of them has to be smashed into a paste with the heel of a shoe, then that must be at least something to be wary of. If it happens every time such a creature appears, then the developing psyche has no choice but to recognise the creatures as a definite threat to life itself. The response is embedded into the reptilian complex and, when triggered, is under way before we know about it and instantly becomes self-cycling.

It's not always set by example. An anxious reaction from an elder to something their child is doing can be enough; if an elder is frightened of it, then the child will perceive that there is obviously a risk of harm. Here are some examples:

- **When seeing a child studying a spider:** 'Oh no, don't touch it! It'll run up your arm and get stuck in your ear and you'll have to go to hospital!'; a double whammy here, creating a fear of spiders and hospitals in one fell swoop.

- **When a child picks up an earthworm or some other harmless creature:** 'Aargh! Put it down! It's covered in germs and will make you ill!'

- **Speaking about something threatening in front of a child:** 'Honestly, you can't go anywhere without somebody trying to stick a knife in you.' Just a rather exaggerated observation of course, but a developing psyche can easily take it literally and develop such a reaction as agoraphobia.

- **Reacting to a child's illness with evident anxiety and excessive comforting, especially to vomiting:** This can create emetophobia (one of the most difficult phobic responses to release).

At this point, if you yourself have children, you might now be realising that you've already created quite a bit of conditioning as a result of your own conditioned responses. It can be tempting to seek to undo any damage with a comforting conversation and assurance that these things are not really that dangerous and it's just that you're a bit silly sometimes. Well it will make you feel better, that's for sure, but as to whether it will decondition the response is a matter of wait and see. Of course, if your reparation speech doesn't have the desired effect you can always introduce them to this book later on. The most important thing if you're in this category is to not beat yourself up – you didn't choose to be how you are and neither did those who taught you. It's fair to say, though, that not everybody subject to conditioning ends up with a phobia and it does depend on a great many factors as to who does and who does not. It seems to have little to do with the level of intelligence and might be related to how impressionable or intuitive a child is – the more a child can sense the meaning behind the parent's reaction, the more they will be likely to learn the same response the parent has. In this way, fear begets fear; confidence begets confidence. It's certainly the case that many, if not most, people with a phobia will report that their mother/father/uncle/aunt/grandmother etc. was just the same.

Dealing with it

It matters not one bit if, at this point, you're thinking to yourself that nobody in your family has ever exhibited a phobia, so conditioning cannot have been the cause. It might be the case that you've acquired the fear via some other route, or simply forgotten about the person of influence who managed to introduce you to the idea. School teachers of very young children are frequently a person of influence; after all, they're a teacher – so they must know even more than our parents, right? The fact is, you have it (wherever it came from), and now it's time to start looking at how to get rid of it. There are two important elements to consider first:

1. Make sure it's a simple phobia, i.e. whatever it is that sets you off is not truly likely to kill you. Some might argue that almost anything can kill you given the right circumstances, but for our purposes we'll say that a one-in-a-million chance doesn't count as likely so it can be included here.

2. Investigate what you think or fear might happen if you encountered the trigger; if you can't think of anything, make it up – even if it's ridiculous. This is not intended to cure the problem (it definitely won't do that) but to condition the reptilian complex into searching for what might make it feel better. Without this step, there's a chance that a subconscious resistance would seek to avoid change.

As you are probably expecting, we need to create the New You as well as the Ideal Future, but we're going to work slightly differently in this procedure – you'll have to do a little mental juggling here but the results will be worth it. To create the New You, think about how you would prefer to feel when encountering the phobic situation: as relaxed as when watching a favourite TV programme, for example; perhaps the same as when you're reading a magazine or lazing in the park. It can be anything you like and doesn't have to be connected to the phobia because it's just to identify a feeling for the reptilian complex. You might have already worked out that this is okay because whatever is causing your phobic response, it's not dangerous so you can afford to be extremely relaxed about it – it doesn't matter one jot that you can't imagine feeling like that when faced with your phobia. Once you've found it, move outside of it so you see how you look in your mind's eye (or you can just think of how you would look instead). Although that's really an other you, it's the New You as far as the phobia is concerned. Be sure it's an active image – i.e. you doing something – because that's what's needed in the procedure. Your Ideal Future will be created within the procedure itself this time.

Only continue when you've understood all that you've read in this chapter so far, even if you've disagreed with parts of it (which will cause no problem of any sort).

The procedure

As long as you can understand the notion of conditioning and how it happens, all necessary preparation has now been done – even if you're not too sure about that. The procedure you'll be completing here is effectively a double-deconditioning process (there are two sets of repeats) and as long as you can complete each step of the procedure successfully, the chances of a permanent and full release from the phobic response are very high. Your level of concentration and imagination comes into it a little – so when you've managed to completely dissolve the problem, you're allowed to give yourself a pat on the back and boast a little. The recorded version of the therapy is pretty much essential here.

1. Bring the phobia situation to mind and make it feel as bad as you can handle so that you might even be able to feel the usual response starting.

2. Immediately Stop and Stare the scene to completely stop every bit of the response. If it doesn't stop immediately, stare harder until it does.

3. Imagine a cartoon drawing of the same scene but without you in it – this is the seed for the Ideal Future.

4. Close your eyes to continue with the Virtual Reality section:

- Focus on the stopped image.
- Immediately block it with the active New You image looking absolutely at ease.
- See thousands of flashes of neural pathways lighting up in the brain in the front, back, left, right, whole brain, as you count to five at 1-second intervals.
- Stare at the cartoon Ideal Future until it becomes active.
- See a cartoon image of the New You walking into that Ideal Future.

5. Repeat step 4 five more times, as quickly as you can.

6. Now the cartoon image suddenly becomes real life as you zoom right into it.

7. Actually feel that New You in that Ideal future.

8. See thousands of flashes of neural pathways lighting up in the brain in the front, back, left, right, whole brain, as you count to five at one-second intervals.

9. Repeat steps 7–8 five more times.

10. Drift down into the reptilian complex and into the Super Unwind – Part Two (see page 22).

11. Once back up to full awareness, check the PAL of the trigger again; repeat the procedure once or twice if the score is higher than 3 – this often won't be necessary.

Text to record

1. 'Bring the phobia into your mind and make it feel as bad as you can take, even so you begin to feel the usual feeling.' (5-second pause)

2. (Urgently) 'Now Stop and Stare the whole scene so every bit of everything just stops. Stare harder to make absolutely certain.' (2-second pause)

3. 'Now imagine a cartoon drawing of the same scene, still stopped and without you in it.' (2-second pause)

4. (Intensely) 'Now focus on that stopped image and immediately block it with the moving image of the New You looking completely relaxed.'

5. (Not too fast from here) 'And see thousands of flashes of neural pathways lighting up all over the brain in the front, back, left, right, whole brain, while you count to five.' (5-second pause)

6.   'Now stare at the cartoon drawing in your mind again and see it suddenly become active and you realise this really is your Ideal Future.'

7.   'And now see a cartoon image of you walking into that Ideal Future.'

Repeat steps 4–7 five more times as quickly as you can, then continue straight away with the next section, speaking quickly and urgently:

8.   'And now that cartoon version of the Ideal Future suddenly becomes real life and you zoom right into the very heart of it to actually become the New You.'

9.   'Now you can actually feel that New You in that fantastic Ideal Future.'

10. 'And you can see thousands of flashes of neural pathways lighting up in your brain in the front, back, left, right, whole brain, as you count to five.' (5-second pause)

Repeat steps 9 and 10 five more times, speaking quickly and urgently, then continue immediately into:

11. 'And now drift down into the reptilian complex and into the Super Unwind – Part Two.'

That's the end of the recording and, when you're back to full awareness, instead of testing for the PAL (phobias are almost always reported as a 10) revisit the original scene and notice the improvement. It's entirely possible that you'll discover there is no phobic response at all, though if it's still noticeable you can repeat the process the next day.

First aid tip

If you should feel a ripple or two, you'll be able to restore calm very quickly by closing your eyes and repeating the following step from the procedure:

▪ See hundreds of flashes of neural pathways lighting up in the brain in the front, back, left, right, whole brain, as you count to five at 1-second intervals.

Now we're ready to move on to the complex phobia.

Chapter 12

The Complex Phobia

The complex phobia isn't a phobia at all in the truest sense of the word, even if it feels like it might be. It's not defined by the amount of fear, or type of reaction, which can be every bit as profound as in the simple phobia. The individual might faint, hyperventilate, vomit, sob, run away, be in sudden need of a lavatory or any of the myriad responses seen in many of the simple phobias.

> The defining feature is whether or not it potentially poses a genuine threat.

The simple phobia is based around a trigger where there is minimal risk (or no risk at all) of any harm. The complex phobia is always associated with a recognisable risk that is impossible to refute, so it is at least partly rational. To clarify this statement:

- A mouse cannot cause you any harm; a crane fly cannot cause any harm; a house spider cannot cause any harm: these are elements of a simple phobia.
- Aeroplanes do crash and kill people; fatal accidents happen on fast roads; people do die falling from heights: these are elements of the complex phobia.

When a response is triggered by the sort of event in the second group, the risk to life might not even be consciously recognised – but when it is, the amount of fear is irrational. This is possibly because of a subconscious reversal of possibilities and probabilities. For instance, an aeroplane can possibly crash but probably won't; if you reverse *possibly* and *probably* it's easy to see where the fear comes from. But all the aerophobic individual knows is that they are too terrified to get on an aeroplane – or to get on one that is going to take off and fly, anyway. Somewhere, somehow, the reptilian complex has collected the response that flying in an aeroplane is to be avoided at all costs and the rest of the brain does exactly what it's supposed to do – seeks vigorously to avoid danger.

So, since it has the same effect as a simple phobia, why do we even bother to distinguish between the two? Well there is, in fact, a very good reason. We can work directly at the simple phobia because the fear is always about the object of the phobia, but a complex phobia is rarely as direct – in fact, most of the time the situation is far more multifaceted than most people realise. We'll look at two of the most common examples of flying phobia (already touched upon here because it allows clarification so easily, as you'll shortly see) and another common one: driving, especially on motor-ways or in fast-moving traffic. It's worth recognising here that, in the case of the complex phobia, the threat might not necessarily be to do with life or death but to loss of personal integrity – the fear of shame or embarrass-ment or exposure.

Flying fear (aerophobia)

Although some people suffering this phobia can actually fly if they have enough alcohol or tranquilliser, there are many who will freeze at the entrance to the aeroplane (if they even get that far) or have to be removed from their seat as a quivering wreck before the engines have even started. It's easy to imagine that it's because they fear the pilot will lose control, the craft will crash and they and everybody else will die. While that thinking is certainly possible, it's not always the case (although they might not realise it); it can instead be any of these possible associated situations:

- Somebody throwing up/being sick.
- People getting drunk (this response is sometimes associated with emetophobia).
- People starting a fight.
- 'I might get airsick.'
- 'I might need the toilet and not be able to get in.'
- 'I can't eat in front of other people.'
- 'The food might make me ill.'

Any of those events can happen, of course, but they are not in themselves a risk to life and limb. The last four are evidence of the existence of a direct simple phobia response that will possibly be encountered on an aeroplane flight. The first three are themselves indirect phobias (in other words, associated with what somebody else might do – over which you have no control) and therefore of the complex variety and it is the fear of what might happen as a result of encountering them; the root driver of a phobia, be it simple or complex, is always associated totally with self.

The reason these unrecognised associations remain unrecognised most of the time is because of the way the brain works. It's effectively a blanket description effect: these things can happen on an aeroplane and, since one or more of them is at the root of it, if you avoid flying you avoid the risk of encountering any of them.

If you suffer aerophobia, you may have discovered now that it's not what you thought it was, or instead have confirmed the exact opposite – it's exactly what you thought. There's a brief test you can do that will confirm the latter: imagine you knew in advance that not only was the plane not going to crash, but when you landed you would be given whatever it is you want most in life. No conditions. No after-sales pestering. Nothing other than the totally free gift of whatever it is you want most. Would you get on the plane, knowing it was not going to crash? If *yes*, it's the fear of the plane crashing and you simply have an exaggerated belief in the likelihood of a crash. If *no*, then it's something else associated with flying, rather than sudden extinction – which is actually hugely unlikely (though statistics never did cure a phobia, as you've probably already discovered). The good news is that as long as you explore the situation as thoroughly as possible and examine every possibility you can think of, you will have prepared the reptilian complex well enough that your learning here will work exactly as it is designed to do – and probably far better than you might imagine.

Driving fear (amaxophobia)

This situation is similar to aerophobia, where it is easy to imagine that it is all about crashing the car and dying as a result. Sometimes that is the case and it can be so total that the person cannot drive at all under any circumstances; or it might be only motorways (*freeways* in the USA) or fast roads that trigger the response. The unrecognised possibilities here are:

- 'Someone might lose control and crash into me.'

- 'Someone might cause an accident right in front of me and I won't know what to do.'

- 'Someone might cause an accident and I could get the blame.'

- 'I might lose control and cause an accident.'

- 'I might make a stupid mistake and damage my car.'

- 'I might do something wrong and get picked up by the police.'

- 'The car might suddenly do something I don't understand.'

Once again, the first three are associated with fears about what others might do; the remainder are about the individual being inept. They are quite specific here and can refer to any aspect of life; losing control, doing something stupid, doing something wrong, not understanding – all (or any) of which could have dire consequences in other situations as well as driving. Again, the brain is doing its blanket description trick: 'these things can happen while driving, so avoiding driving minimises the risk'. As with aerophobia, it doesn't matter what the underlying cause is – as long as you investigate every possibility you can think of, you will condition the reptilian complex for positive change.

All complex phobias

If you have either aerophobia or amaxophobia, you now hopefully have a clearer view of the possibilities surrounding them – but if it's something else that plagues you, don't worry because the same rules apply for all complex phobias. There is a risk that will have somehow become inflated in your mind and there will almost certainly also be one, or a few, unrecognised undercurrents. It doesn't matter whether it's the fear of heights ('somebody might push me off', 'I might throw myself off', 'The wind might blow me over' and more); speaking in public ('They might laugh at me', 'I might say something stupid', 'I might need the lavatory' and similar); escalators ('I might get my foot trapped', 'I might fall', 'Somebody in the crowd might shove me over' and the like) or anything else – there are always unrecognised possibilities lurking beneath them.

Now do as shown in the sections on aerophobia and amaxophobia – write down half-a-dozen or more possibilities, including at least three that might be the result of somebody else's behaviour or mistake. It doesn't matter in the least if you think they don't really apply to you; it doesn't even truly matter if one or two of them seem rather stupid or unlikely – it's all about getting your reptilian complex out of its current state and ready to accept beneficial change. There are a couple more important concepts to consider first, before getting into the procedure that will sort it all out.

Imagination

Complex phobias engender a particular response from some others that is usually absent in the case of the simple phobia. In the latter, there will often be irritated remarks such as 'what on earth do you suppose it could do to you?' or 'for goodness sake – they're more scared of you than you are of them.' The complex phobia, though, produces something entirely different: the vehement statistician. Now, the use of statistics can be beneficial but only under certain circumstances – and not when they are delivered with an air of superiority, or with the apparent aim of convincing the phobic individual of their inability to bring logic to bear on the issue. The fact is that in any battle between logic and imagination, imagination will always win. You can be shown a hundred articles that say the greatest risk is on the drive to the airport, not on the flight, and all that happens is that you might add a phobia of road travel to the one about flying. Or you might be told that there is only one accident per gazillion trips on an escalator; maybe about the rigorous multifaceted testing of lifts before they are allowed to be in service. Or perhaps the millions of hours of safety testing of modern motor vehicles before they're allowed to go on the market. Whether these facts were already known or if they were new information, they make not the slightest difference; the fact that there is a chance of disaster, no matter how slight, is enough to convince the owner of a phobia that the risk to them is greater, even if nobody else can see that fact. Imagination has won the day, as it always does. It doesn't matter that millions of aeroplane flights daily are without incident; hearing about one flying into a mountainside and exploding can grip the mental imagery of some people like a vice. And paralysing anxiety after hearing that a bat got entangled in somebody's hair, for example, is not relieved by being told that it probably didn't really happen, because it did in the mind of the chiroptophobic (chiroptophobia is the fear of bats). But it is that very process – imagination – that also allows the effective resolution of the complex phobia.

Conditioning

We looked at this subject in Chapter 11 but the process is different for the complex phobia, so here it is again. The type of conditioning here is based, more often than not, on the anxieties of the person of influence; be that a parent, grandparent, teacher or other individual with an air of authority or a tone of voice that somehow conveys their superior status. Because the authoritative one is already anxious, they increase the level of perceived threat to the point of wild exaggeration and it's the sense of urgency that does the damage:

- Saying, 'Be careful! Hold on tight to the bannisters or you'll fall and break your neck!' to a child on some stairs.
- Saying, 'Don't touch it! It might bite your hand off!' to a child on encountering a dog.
- Saying, 'No, we can't go to Spain – we'd have to go on a plane and it's too dangerous.'
- Saying, 'If you go near the window you'll get struck by lightning' during a thunderstorm.

The possible result of those statements is obvious and the same thing could happen if the child sees an adult behaving fearfully in those situations. However, just as with simple phobias, it's not clear what creates a phobic response in one child while another one just laughs, and yet another decides to test the concept as soon as they can. It seems clear that the more imaginative an individual is, the more clearly they can form mind pictures – but again, that's often the very process that allows us to finally resolve the issue.

If you realise you have inadvertently created a phobia in your child, the advice given in Chapter 11 is also valid here.

Dealing with it

There are a few concepts that are important to logically agree with before we can move on to the procedure for this chapter. It's not intended that logical understanding will in any way lessen or cure the phobic response – if that were even possible, you probably would not have the problem in the first place. The reason for this step is simply to ensure that the relevant neural threads in the reptilian complex have been activated; an essential aspect if we are to find success. All the following statements are true and it is probable that they have been stated to you more than once – but that was by somebody trying to force a change of mind onto you (no matter how they described it); here, however, it is just stated as a matter of fact for you to confirm your understanding before we get to work. If you find yourself with a 'yes but … ' response, search within to see if part of you is seeking to maintain the phobic response. If so then you already have what you want and, while this chapter will have given you a greater understanding of its source, it is unlikely to release the response if you don't want it to. Here are the concepts needing logical agreement:

- Statistics about events, situations and objects are not about people but about the events, situations and objects. Since they are not about people, they are the same for everybody as long as relevant instructions for use are being followed.

- Everything we do has some element of risk; even lying in bed all the time to avoid risk increases the likelihood of cardiovascular problems (among others). Electricity and gas can both kill but avoiding both would increase the risk to health for a variety of reasons, including hygiene.

- Natural phenomena, such as storms and floods, occur everywhere but you would not be able to attract one to your area if your life depended on it.

- This one's a question rather than a statistic: aeroplanes do sometimes crash and there are more than 100,000 flights made every day. So how much money would you bet on any one particular flight crashing – say, the one leaving London's Heathrow for New York at 11.30 am tomorrow morning? Would you expect to win or lose the bet?

Okay, you're probably unimpressed with the statistics but the more information your reptilian complex has, the better it can work for you. Now, as far as resolving the phobia is concerned, the procedure here is somewhat different from what you have seen so far and is particularly well-suited to the task – it is, though, a little more complicated. You can if you wish, however, use either the one from Chapter 3 or Chapter 11 instead.

This version is different in that we don't employ an Ideal Future; instead, just working with the New You is the best method for the complex phobia. This is because the complex phobia is almost always associated with something with which we have an input – some measure of control. Creating an Ideal Future means you could feel that the phobia was still existent until you experienced the phobic situation again – and for some individuals that could create doubt, which can inhibit the success you will otherwise experience. Now you just have to construct the New You by creating a phrase from the two word lists, as you've done before. The word lists are reproduced again here; remember to choose one word from each group and link them together with *and* or *but* as necessary to make a coherent phrase:

Set 1	Set 2
enthusiastic	cautious
relaxed	careful
energised	aware
relieved	watchful
happy	accepting
calm	sensible
confident	tolerant
at ease	

Choose the two that work best for you; it matters not one jot whether you believe that you could ever feel like that in the phobia situation – you've not done the procedure yet. Think of some time when you've felt like that (it doesn't need to be in any way connected with the phobia) and see yourself, as if from the outside, in that exact situation. Make it vivid in your mind and notice the feeling in your body and mind at the same time.

The procedure

This is a little more complicated than you are used to, but is capable of outstanding results. As with the simple phobia procedure, it really does need the recorded option.

1. Think about how you are now, with whatever phobia it is you have: this is your current self. See yourself, as if from the outside, in the phobia situation and make it look like an old black-and-white film or video. If it gets too uncomfortable, Stop and Stare the image to quieten it.

2. Look at it as if from the outside looking in, then from the inside looking out. Do that a few times, pausing for 1 second between each change, so: looking in (1-second pause), looking out (1-second pause) and so on, until it's easy – it might only take three changes. Finish on the inside looking out.

3. Now see the New Self as if from the outside, in Ultra HD full-colour video, in the same phobia situation but looking absolutely [*insert chosen phrase*]. Do the same switching process as before with a 1-second pause between each change, and again practise until it's so easy you can choose to be inside looking out or outside looking in.

4. Now be inside the black-and-white video looking out.

5. Jump out so that you can see it from the outside looking in and Stop and Stare it to stop it.

6. The instant it has stopped, swap it for the Ultra HD full-colour video.

7. Immediately drop into it as the New Self to be on the inside looking out.

8. Actually feel the New Self feeling [*insert chosen phrase*] in your body.

9. See thousands of flashes of neural pathways lighting up in the brain as they carry the [*insert chosen phrase*] feeling to the front, back, left, right, whole brain, as you count to five at 1-second intervals.

10. Repeat steps 4–9 quickly.

11. Drift down into the reptilian complex and into the Super Unwind – Part Two (see page 22).

12. Once back up to full awareness, check the PAL of the trigger again and repeat the procedure once or twice if the PAL is higher than 3 – this often won't be necessary.

Text to record

You need to complete steps 1–3 from the procedure first, taking as long as you need, then start your recording and close your eyes, continuing with speed and intensity. The text to record is:

1. 'Imagine you're on the inside of the black-and-white video, as if you're looking out from a black-and-white world.'

2. 'Now jump out of there so you can see it from the outside looking in and immediately Stop and Stare it to stop it dead.' (2-second pause)

3. 'Now swap it over for the Ultra HD full-colour video and make it vivid as you immediately drop into it as the New Self to be on the inside looking out from a full-colour world.'

4. 'Actually feel the New Self feeling [*insert chosen phrase*] in your body.'

5.	'Now see thousands of flashes of neural pathways lighting up in your brain as they carry the [*insert chosen phrase*] feeling to the front, back, left, right, whole brain, as you count to five.' (5-second pause)

Repeat steps 1–5, speaking quickly and with emphasis, then continue:

6.	'Now drift down into the reptilian complex and into the Super Unwind – Part Two.'

That's the end of the recording; when you're back to full awareness it's entirely possible that you'll discover there is no phobic response at all (again, we're not using the PAL test), though if it's still noticeable you can repeat the process the next day.

First aid tip

Again, as for the simple phobia, if you should feel a ripple or two, you'll be able to restore calm very quickly by closing your eyes and repeating the following step from the procedure:

■	See hundreds of flashes of neural pathways lighting up in the brain in the front, back, left, right, whole brain, as you count to five at 1-second intervals.

Now for something completely different.

Chapter 13

Performance Enhancement

Performance enhancement always has to incorporate psychology, whatever the field you want to improve performance in – and a major part of it comes back to something you've read about before in this book: belief. This means that once you learn the trick, you can improve performance in anything you choose using the programme here. Of course, belief is not the only aspect of performance enhancement but it is one of the most important, even when working with physicality (such as in sports).

Belief, in fact, underpins a huge amount of what we do and what we can achieve but it is an astonishingly fragile concept that is prone to change, according to circumstances. It is an indisputable fact that having a high belief that you can succeed at something enhances your chances of success. It is also an indisputable fact that if you believe you cannot succeed then you probably won't. The famous quote by Henry Ford, reported in 1947, is absolutely correct:

'Whether you think you can, or you think you can't – you're right.'[1]

There are two important aspects of belief. The first is that it comes in different strengths – you can believe 100 per cent in something or you can half-believe something, or almost believe – which usually means you believe, but only a little bit. The second important aspect is that you cannot easily change your level of belief without some other input; you either

---

1 S. Cassidy, "Whether You Think You Can, or You Think You Can't – You're Right." *Advance HE* [blog] (n.d.). Available at: https://www.heacademy.ac.uk/%E2%80%9Cwhether-you-think-you-can-or-you-think-you-cant-youre-right%E2%80%9D.

believe something at a certain level or you don't, and you can't just decide to change that belief in either direction. Here's a simple illustration of how easily your belief system can change with an extra piece of information and how it's also linked to resolve – another hugely important concept for performance enhancement:

- Imagine a small room, around three metres square, with the floor strewn with small pieces of hay. You are told that there might be a sewing needle in there somewhere and offered £5 if you can find it. Think about how enthusiastically you would look for it and for how long.

- Again, imagine the same small room with the floor strewn with small pieces of hay. This time you observe somebody tossing a sewing needle in there, though you don't see where it lands. You are offered £5,000 if you can find it. Think about how enthusiastically you would look for it and for how long.

In the first instance, you would probably give up quite quickly (though it would depend on how much you needed the £5). In the second instance, you would have no doubt in believing that the needle was there to be found, though your residual belief system triggered by the phrase *like looking for a needle in a haystack* might work against your belief that you could find it. You would almost certainly look for longer in the second instance and in both cases the length of time you spent looking would be (to an extent) dictated by your level of resolve, by how much you needed the reward and by the possibilities of what you could do with it.

You can already begin to see how important belief and resolve are, but we're not finished yet because motivation is also involved (the £5 or £5,000). Sometimes resolve is mistakenly confused with motivation, but they are not the same thing at all. You might have any one of the three elements without the other two, but unless you have all three working together you are effectively running uphill in the pursuit of any form of success. *Motivation* is what inspires you to pursue a goal (in this case, enhance your performance in one area or another); *belief* governs how much *resolve* you will have to achieve that goal – remove any one of the three and you can see the problem. Conversely, you can have all three by the bucket-load and yet not stand even the slightest chance of success – usually when the belief is unfounded. For instance, an individual reads an internet post stating that by following a special plan that's literally *ready to go, out of the box* they can earn more money than a brain surgeon working only two days a week. They believe the testimonial stories of ordinary people who have become near-millionaires in one month via the same plan and so they are motivated to sign up, full of resolve to give it everything they've got. Unfortunately, they've never run a website and they don't have a mailing list; both of which turn out to be pre-requisites for the plan and not anywhere near as easy to acquire as the promotional internet post indicated. Then they discover they don't have enough money to buy the mailing list and have the website built; as time passes, resolve fades, motivation disappears completely and belief in the project is now at zero.

The element that was missing in the plan is something that is absolutely vital if you're in pursuit of just about any goal when you're bringing outside influences into your sphere of existence. Until now, in this book, we've worked at various different issues but they've all been self-contained; that is, using thoughts and processes that you've already had in the past to bring about a change in response to certain situations. Here, though, you're looking at the idea of moving beyond your current state to improve your performance in some activity – it doesn't matter what.

The missing element is the main reason for a failure: not checking the suitability of the plan for you and your resources.

This is so important that BWRT professionals always check an idea is plausible, possible and fair (PPF) – and they usually refer to it as *2PF*. What this means is that whatever is being sought must be possible, it must be plausible for you and it must be fair to give it the best chance. For instance, it's possible to run 100 metres in 10 seconds but it's not plausible for somebody with arthritic knees. And fair? Well, in this context, that means the sought-after goal is entirely for your benefit and not to punish or hurt somebody else. It's fair if you want to enhance your ability at playing pool because you want to win more games, but not if it's mainly because you want to make somebody else feel jealous or put them in their place. This is because the reptilian complex works best with the broadest aims – winning more games overall is broader than wanting to beat one person. Not only that but, if you're focusing on somebody else losing, your reptilian complex might focus on losing instead of winning; if it's not fair, you might get away with it and you might not – but 2PF is safest.

So, you need motivation, belief, resolve and a 2PF test – the exact formula used by the professional therapists. And now here's a questionnaire to complete, the result of which will show the likelihood of success; again, this is very similar to the questionnaire a BWRT practitioner might use. It's best to write your answers down before looking at what they all mean:

1. What is it that you want to be able to do?

2. What stops you being able to do that anyway?

3. Were you ever able to do it?

   a. If *yes*: what caused you to stop being able to do that?

   b. If *no*: how do you know you are capable of doing that now?

4. What would have to happen before you could do that?

5. What might stop you being able to achieve that?

It's essential not to rush the answers because the questionnaire is an important part of performance enhancement and the more complete your response, the greater the likelihood of success. Not only that but, once they have been properly processed and adjusted if necessary, they will have played an important part in reorganising the way your reptilian complex responds in relation to your stated goal. Time – and thought – spent answering each question as fully as possible will pay huge dividends later, especially if you do that conscientiously and before reading on past this sentence (it is a fact that if you look at the way the answers are processed, you will cheat – even if you don't recognise it; then you'll be fooling yourself).

The likelihood score

Okay, last chance – if you've not written down all your answers yet, do so before reading on to get the best possible performance enhancement. If you're definitely ready to continue though, here we go with an analysis of your answers. Write your score next to each one, since you'll need that shortly. We're using a 0–3 scale here, unlike the 1–10 of the PAL:

1. If your goal is clearly 100 per cent for you and you alone, score it as a 3. If there is also an element where you are seeking to in some way defeat another individual known to you (but not somebody with whom you have no personal connection) score it at 2. If you now realise there's an ulterior motive and it's not really 2PF, score it at 0 – in which case you can optionally continue or reappraise your goal (recommended).

2. If your answer here is definitely a mindset problem, such as destructive or limiting thoughts, it scores 3. If it's a physical skill

difficulty, then score it at 2. If it's a problem with your body's structure or proportions, score it at 1.

3. (a): If it was a mind problem, such as loss of confidence or onset of doubt, it's a 3. If you don't really know or cannot remember, score it as 2; if it was a change in physiology (the way your body works, for example) it's a 1.

    (b): If it would make sense to everybody, it's a rational response and the score is 1; otherwise, score it at 0.

4. If it would make sense to everybody straight away, it's a 3. If you don't know, it's 2 and if it makes sense only to you, it's doubtful, so a 0.

5. If it would make sense to everybody, it's 3. If you don't know, give it a 2 and if it would only make sense to you, it's a 1.

The highest possible score is 15, the lowest possible score (not including 0) is 5; any answer scoring 0 indicates the need for a great deal of thought and a possible reworking of your ideas, maybe even an abandonment of the plan, unless you can find a valid answer. Also, 0-scoring answers to (2) and (3) are going to be severely limiting; although it might be possible to overcome such physiological limitations, it is probably beyond the scope of this book. In general, the further away from the maximum score, the more effort will be needed – but this doesn't mean that you cannot be successful, only that you have to give it your very best shot.

It's essential to recognise two particular elements of performance enhancement that often elude people; if these two elements are ignored, the chances of success are weakened. The first is that whatever method you are using (whether it's BWRT or the *brute force* method of *practice, practice, practice*) it's not a *set it and forget it* process. You need to keep at it to achieve it and you need to keep at it to sustain it, whatever it is (sustained application is always needed, which is why so few people manage to clamber to the top in any field). The second element to be aware of – wary of, even – is that performance enhancement means change. Change is all-encompassing; change one part of your life and it will impact on something else somewhere. Currently, the way your life works has a particular balance. It might not be perfect but it's a balance you are used to and the result of pursuing performance enhancement will almost certainly involve a bit of rebalancing. It can change your relationships with others quite markedly, for instance, whether or not they are involved in whatever performance you are seeking to enhance. Jealousy can rear its head at the least opportunity sometimes.

Motivation and resolve

It's assumed here that you have a sufficiently high level of belief and motivation to achieve your goal (because since you're still reading, you have probably not been put off by what you've read so far), so all that's necessary for the practical aspects of the work here is to examine your resolve. It's not possible to discover the level of that particular resource via a questionnaire, so it needs a bit of thought experimentation to determine. Resolve is linked to belief so if you truly believe you can achieve, the higher your resolve will be and the more it will take to stop you. Remember the room with the hay and the needle earlier in this chapter; if you knew it was there, your belief and resolve would be far higher. So, if you believe beyond doubt that it's: (a) possible for somebody to do it, (b) plausible for you to do it, and (c) totally focused on you – in other words, if it's fully 2PF – then your resolve should be sky-high. If a *but* is now in your mind, it means, of course, that there are other circumstances to take into account and you are the only one who can assess the likelihood of them getting in your way. Here are some common circumstances to carefully consider:

- **Financial considerations:** Much of the time, performance enhancement is more dependent on time than money – but not always. There might be outlay needed for training or relevant equipment, for instance, or maybe website development. Whatever it is, you need to ensure there are sufficient funds to avoid a shortfall wrecking your plans after you've already invested time and energy. If it's not feasible to ensure enough finance, then your plan fails at the second P – it's not totally plausible. Back to the drawing board to modify your plan to fit within your financial circumstances.

- **Time constraints:** Where the enhancement is primarily in processes of thought, such as an increased presence during webinar presentations, for instance, then no extra time is likely to be needed. But where there is a physical improvement sought – running faster, jumping higher, throwing further, for example – then the body will need to practise developing the musculature and coordination the changed thought processes will make possible. Ensure you have taken the extra training time needed into account – or it's back to the drawing board.

- **Resistance from others:** The most difficult one. Even when your plan is 2PF, other people can get in the way. This might be because, when you decide to improve any aspect of yourself, they are jealous, resentful, critical or even downright unpleasant – for any number of reasons. They won't necessarily be so, of course, but it's certainly a possibility, especially if they feel you are moving up a notch or are elevating yourself above them in some way (though they'll be likely to say anything but that). There are two options here: (1) don't tell anybody and leave them guessing when your plan pays off; or (2) tell them and resolve that if they try to put you off, it's about them and not you.

Important: only move on from this point when you are sure that you have assimilated and put into practice all that you have read so far.

Doing it

The best procedure for performance enhancement is a version of the standard process you learned in Chapter 3, so we're using that here. You'll need to create the New You and also the Ideal Future (obviously in relation to your particular performance enhancement). We'll be using the PAL measurement in a slightly different way than usual, to give a clear indication of the level of success the procedure has achieved. You're also going to use a different process to find the New You this time; instead of selecting words from lists, a method often referred to as *modelling* is being used here. The first thing to do is imagine somebody who is able to perform at the level you are aiming for. What you need here is not just an imaginary person, but an actual individual that you know of (it doesn't matter if you know them personally or they are a public figure of some sort). Now here's a mini procedure to get everything ready for the main event – this one doesn't need to be recorded to work well.

Mini procedure

1. Create a mental video of them performing and vividly imagine how you would feel in your mind and body if it were you in that scene instead of them.

2. Stop and Stare the mental video and imagine it's you who you're looking at instead of them.

3. See yourself from the outside, looking as if you can feel everything you need; confidence, belief, assurance, positivity.

4.   Now zoom in to become that New You for a moment.

5.   Repeat steps 3–4 five times, staying longer in the moment each time – finish with you on the outside, looking at a still image of the scene.

That simple process is all that some performance enhancement therapies would use, but we have much to do yet that will provide something many times stronger, starting with the creation of a placeholder for the Ideal Future. This is the easy bit: imagine a still image of you involved in your performance; like a photograph, but with your back to the camera. Even though you can't see your features, there is something about this photo that clearly shows the performance enhancement procedure has done its job.

The procedure

Remember, you can record all – or part – of this and listen to it to get the very best results; the closest self-help possible to a session with a professional therapist.

1.   Bring a vivid image to mind of you involved in whatever performance you are seeking to enhance, seeing yourself as you are now. Be sure to visualise and feel the frustration or disappointment that has led you to seek to improve the performance, and get the PAL (the greater the frustration or disappointment, the higher the score).

2.   Stop and Stare the image.

3.   Immediately move into the Virtual Reality section:
   ● Focus on the stopped image.
   ● Immediately block it with the New You image.
   ● Focus on the feeling of the New You in your body.
   ● See thousands of flashes of neural pathways lighting up in the brain.
   ● Dive into the placeholder of the Ideal Future to become the New You.
   ● The Ideal Future immediately becomes active and you are on the inside feeling part of it all and feeling exactly as you want to feel; the same confidence, belief, assurance, positivity that you accessed earlier.

4.   Repeat step 3 five more times.

5.   Drift down into the reptilian complex and into the Super Unwind – Part Two (see page 22).

6. Once back up to full awareness, check the PAL – but this time of the level of confidence, belief, assurance and positivity. Subtract this from the original PAL (of frustration, disappointment, etc.); where the new score is above 3 you can run through the procedure again on subsequent days. Once it's below 3, you can revisit as necessary – though only running the procedure once a day.

Text to record

1. 'Imagine you can see yourself doing [*say the activity you want to enhance*] as you are at the moment. Make sure you can feel the frustration or disappointment about it and get the PAL.' (5-second pause)

2. 'Stop and Stare the image so that it's frozen in time.' (2-second pause)

3. 'Now focus vividly on that stopped image and immediately block it with the moving image of the New You.'

4. 'Focus on the feeling of the New You as thousands of flashes of neural pathways begin to light up all over your brain.'

5. 'Those flashes become the brightest as you dive into that placeholder of the Ideal Future to become the New You.'

6. 'The Ideal Future immediately becomes active and you zoom right in to be a real part of it all, feeling exactly as you want to feel with the same confidence, belief, assurance, positivity and everything that you saw in your mind earlier.'

Repeat steps 3–6 five more times, then continue:

7. 'Now drift down into the reptilian complex and into the Super Unwind – Part Two.'

That's the end of the recording and once you're back up to full awareness, open your eyes and check the PAL – but this time the level of confidence, belief, assurance and positivity. Subtract this from the original PAL (of frustration, disappointment, etc.) to give you a new score, as shown in the procedure. Ideally, you will run this procedure a few times a month for a while, until you are unable to create an image that is more successful than you have already become – meaning that you have reached your (currently possible) peak. When this happens, forget all about it until the day you once again discover the desire to improve on your performance.

Chapter 14

Dealing with Mild to Moderate Depression

Depression is one of those situations, like anxiety, that most people experience at some point in their lives and it often has its roots in the same stressors that trigger anxiety.[1] One also often follows the other, too. Before progressing any further, the same advice given in Chapter 10 is in order since vitamin deficiency can also be at the root of depression:

If you've not been tested for medical causes of anxiety – particularly for issues with your thyroid gland and deficiency in vitamins D3 and B12 – then it would be a good idea to request these from your GP, along with a check for other possible causes (such as autoimmune disorders) before continuing with the material here.

Assuming you have already been down that route, you might have been prescribed antidepressants which you should not discontinue without your GP's guidance – even in the event that what you're reading here lifts your spirits well enough for you to begin to enjoy life again. The success of this procedure does depend, to an extent, on what type of depression you have; there are two main types, though there are also several sub-types which

---

1   T. Tjornehoj, The Relationship Between Anxiety and Depression, *Hartgrove Behavioural Health System* [blog] (n.d.). Available at: https://www.hartgrovehospital.com/relationship-anxiety-depression/.

are beyond the scope of this book – including lethargic depression, which is usually part of a personality disorder. These are the two most common:

- **Reactive:** Something has created the depressed state and even if you don't know what it is, you can probably remember when it started. It can almost always be lifted and this book is likely to do just that.
- **Endogenous:** This feels as if it's somehow built in to your psyche. It's been there a long time and doesn't change much, either for better or worse. It can improve greatly but may not lift altogether.

In this book we're working only with reactive depression. It is possible that what is written here will help with endogenous depression a little, but it's not really designed for that. A quick and fairly accurate test to see which type you have is to ask yourself whether or not you have ever felt worse or better than you do at this moment. If 'yes' you are likely to have the reactive form (it doesn't matter whether or not you can remember what triggered it). If 'no' then you are more likely to be experiencing the endogenous form, which used to be known by its old-fashioned title of *melancholia*.

It might come as something of a surprise to realise that it's not unusual for somebody to believe they're depressed, when the reality is that they're experiencing one of these impostors:

- unhappy
- fed up
- stressed
- anxious
- just plain bored

These all have similar components to depression, but usually differ in one important facet: sudden variability. In each of these cases it's entirely possible for events and happenings to trigger a sudden lift of mood to, at the very least, an acceptable level. But when the depression is real, the emotional responses themselves are depressed and almost completely inactive or dormant. The first two – *unhappy* and *fed up* – might respond well to the two procedures in this chapter; the next two – *stressed* and *anxious* – will be much improved by the material in Chapters 8, 9 and 10. The final one – *just plain bored* – well, although it might not make much sense, the material in Chapter 7 (on boosting your self-worth) can improve matters a lot; this is because your personal confidence will improve and therefore allow the reptilian complex to respond positively to a wider range of stimuli.

A tricky situation

Depression often brings with it one of the most difficult situations to resolve (one which can severely hamper any attempt to get free from it); it is the rather odd and completely irrational wish to maintain it, along with flat resistance to anything designed to release it. It's seldom a conscious process and the individual concerned may not even fully realise themselves that they have this process active in their psyche. It's possibly associated with being supported by others, which creates the feeling of being in some way special and loved; it might provide an excuse for not being successful (especially when it was caused by not being successful); it could even be the case that it allows the sufferer to opt out of some of the more awkward aspects of life and living.

Whatever the reason, it's revealed in a common response to any suggestion of anything that might help: 'Ah – that wouldn't work for me.' It might not be those exact words, of course – sometimes it's 'Ah, tried that – did nothing for me' or 'I've heard the results don't last', even 'Okay, I might try that at some point' (the polite way of saying 'thanks but no thanks'). All these responses, and others like them, indicate the same thing – a reluctance to try to resolve the issue, though most of the time the individual has no idea why that is. For what we are seeking to do here there's no need to work that out, fortunately. If you're prone to that type of resistance, it's only necessary to admit it to yourself. You don't have to tell anybody – just own up to it in the secrecy of your own mind and resolve to carry on reading anyway. Done that? Excellent.

The human need

You might imagine here that you're going to be reading about love, spiritual support, respect, inclusivity and such – but you're not. While all, or some, of these are important aspects of life for many, they have little to do directly with the existence (or otherwise) of depression. Now we're back to those ancient ancestors again; the ones who did the heavy lifting in the development of an effective reptilian complex. Their lives were far simpler than ours – as are those of all modern animals, other than the human. The basic behaviour programme for most wild animals consists of hunting, eating, sleeping and breeding when possible (for our purposes here we're ignoring fighting or escaping threat). Provided they are able to do those four things on a fairly regular basis, life is just as it should be – they are fulfilling their purpose in life. At the most basic level, it constitutes success – and success, in this instance, is simply surviving long enough to do it all again the next day.

The process by which this basic instinct became tangled up with our modern acquisitive world – with its man-made rules, ethical codes and morals – is too complex to be covered in detail in a self-help book. Suffice to say that those ancient animals didn't search for happiness or the latest gadget; as long as they could hunt, eat, sleep and occasionally mate, their world was as it should be. They didn't really compare themselves with others; their only purpose was to survive from one end of the day to the next and happiness, or any other emotion, didn't really come into it.

The modern human animal is not content with today's versions of that ancient instinctive behaviour (earning money and shopping replaces hunting, eating has to be ever more adventurous, sleeping hasn't changed much and the mating bit is quite severely limited for most) but must still have a purpose if they are to remain at ease in the world. Just surviving doesn't cut it anymore. Survival is relatively easy for the modern human so doesn't constitute a true sense of purpose – but our reptilian complex needs one in order to fulfil its objective. It can sometimes be difficult to define or recognise the sense of purpose; the easiest way to describe it is that it's the main focal point of your life.

You might well have more than one – many do – but the main purpose is almost always to maintain stability in life, just as it was for our ancestors; don't let anything nasty in. When a relatively minor mishap strikes at some part of that focus – say when a business deal goes wrong, a family member transgresses in some way, or a child or pet becomes ill – we experience anxiety and it motivates us to do everything we can to regain stability; then that becomes the new purpose, the new focal point. But if it becomes apparent that this minor mishap is not improving as a result of our efforts, or is even getting worse, we realise the new focal point is itself at risk and begin to lose heart and impetus. That's when we begin to fear the loss of what makes our life what it is and might start to feel there is little point in carrying on – and when the focal point cannot be restored, or is lost completely, we lose interest in the events of everyday life. We stop responding. We are depressed.

Most reactive depression is as a result of the loss of the focal point that was a major part of the stability of our lives. But we have also lost our purpose in life: our reason for actually wanting to stay alive. Because of this we cease to respond to stimulus, which teaches the reptilian complex not to bother us with emotions. And so we feel numb.

We'll be looking at how to deal with this situation soon but if you're feeling that what you've read so far doesn't quite hit the mark for you, you're probably right. And this is where things get a bit complicated as we look at another cause of depression:

- The modern human's hunt is for whatever they discover they need or want.
- They know such things exist because the people who make them tell them so.
- The importance that others attach to these things tells the reptilian complex they are essential to life.
- They therefore have to hunt for the money to exchange for such important things.
- If the hunt fails to produce enough money to acquire the things, it means their hunting skills are insufficient.
- The reptilian complex receives the feedback that the hunting skills are insufficient, which means survival is threatened and so it generates anxiety.
- When the anxiety fails to produce the thing, the reptilian complex ceases to provide stimulus since there is no useful response – and the lack of stimulus equals lack of interest, which equals depression.

Now, before you roll your eyes at the idea that not being able to have the latest phone or television is the cause of depression, it isn't. But the realisation or observation that others seem to have a lot more of everything (even if they actually haven't) might well be. Personality comes into it; an optimist will believe that their life will soon change for the better, while a pessimist might well view it as yet another indicator of their general inferiority. One person might be totally content with what they can have, while another might go on protest marches about inequality of wealth. Some will aspire to amass eye-watering wealth and even build rockets to travel to the edge of Earth's atmosphere, while others will glory in their ability to embrace a frugal *green* life as an example to those floating weightless in a metal tube. For some people, the focus on material goods and general consumerism is somehow a reflection of shallowness, when in fact it is nothing more than evidence of the way the reptilian complex responds to life. As to why one person might be totally unaffected, while another is in despair – well, you'd have to know something of what they were taught about themselves in the early part of their life to understand that one. After all, that's where the reptilian complex gathered most of its information about the self.

There is one other (quite rare) cause of depression and it follows the rule perfectly that depression is the result of a lack of purpose. This is when an individual is massively successful for whatever reason; they have the rare sports car, the mansion in its own estate, the yacht and the private plane, the exclusive designer watch and jewellery, their private tennis court, an infinity pool built into a luxuriously equipped private spa in the aforementioned mansion – everything, in fact, they have ever wanted. Now they have no purpose, no drive, no ambition because they've done it all and have it all.

Sometimes an individual with that sort of wealth finds a new purpose, which might be as diverse as crusading on behalf of an underprivileged section of society or becoming a philanthropist and donating millions – billions, even – to medical research. Or they become depressed enough that they might start to inhale substances to find the lift they used to get from the pursuit of riches, or even decide they don't want to be alive any more. This last origin of depression – great wealth – is certainly beyond the scope of this book (and it is unlikely that such an individual would even be reading it).

Sorting it out

The procedure for working with reactive depression is a little more complicated than for the other issues so far. This is partly because depression makes it difficult to select a valid New You image, since there is little energy to inspire the imagination. For this reason, we will be using the Detachment procedure first, just as the BWRT professionals do, to persuade the psyche that change is possible and desirable. It's followed, a week or so later, with the Energiser procedure. This gentle two-stage shift method has proven to be more effective than seeking to change states from depressed to undepressed in one go. Before we get to that though, there's some important preparation:

1. The past cannot be changed, erased, obliterated or altered in any other way; all that is possible is to change your reaction to it. If

there's something unpleasant that still gives you a problem, deal with it via one of the procedures already covered before continuing – or just accept that it's there and getting further away with every minute of each day.

2. It's important to understand that however things have worked out in the past has no real bearing on how similar things will pan out in the future. If you change on the inside, everything you do changes. Acceptance of this concept is vital for the success of the programme.

3. If there's something you know would have to change before you could be undepressed, it's important to address it via some of the other work in this book before proceeding. If it really cannot be changed for some reason, then you have to accept its presence and improve your life as far as possible, taking that into account.

4. Create a brief description of how the world seems to you. For instance, it might seem cold and grey, like a heavy blanket, like walking through treacle, flat and empty, dark and dreary, etc. If you can't think of anything, accept *dull and drab*. We'll call this the Old World.

5. Finally, create a brief description of how you believe the world feels to those who don't have the experience of depression; vibrant and alive, for example, or bustling, light and energetic, colourful and busy, etc. If you can't think of anything, accept *lively*. It doesn't matter that you cannot feel whatever you have chosen, as long as you can imagine what it looks like. As you've probably guessed, this is the New World.

Genuine agreement with the five concepts listed here is vital if you are to gain lasting relief from depression. If you're finding difficulty or reluctance with any of them, it suggests the resistance mentioned earlier in this chapter – and you can defeat it by determining to understand and resolve whatever the issue is. If you're struggling with steps 4 and/or 5, then all you need to do is to imagine something that represents *dull and drab* and something else that represents *lively* in your mind – but they must genuinely represent those two states. The PAL score isn't used in either of these procedures.

Detachment

Be sure to complete this procedure successfully, then wait for a week or so before moving on to the Energiser. It's definitely best to record and listen to this one to get the best possible effect.

1. Think of some place you'll be going to in a week or so's time; if there isn't anywhere planned, decide where you'll go – even if it's just to the bottom of your street. Anywhere will do as long as it is: (1) away from where you are reading this; and (2) somewhere you don't go to more than once a week, or even have never been to before. Imagine what it would be like if you were there right now, remembering what you're doing today. We'll call this a *memory link*, which will make more sense later.

2. Imagine the Old World image as if you're on the outside looking in.

3. Now imagine you can somehow turn the light off so everything goes dark, and count 5 seconds in your mind.

4. Now turn the light on again and this time you're looking at the New World.

5. Repeat steps 2–4 three or four more times, or until you can confidently switch fairly quickly between the two images: Old World – lights off; lights on – New World. Be sure to finish on New World. It's not important whether or not you can feel the difference at this stage.

6. Eyes closed now. Bring the Old World image to mind and zoom right into it so you can imagine you're really there and even feel it for a count of 3 seconds, then zoom out quickly so that you're on the outside looking in again.

7. Immediately Stop and Stare the image so that nothing is moving by even the tiniest amount. Turn the light off and make it as dark as possible, then turn it on again to see the New World that immediately becomes live and active as you zoom right into the middle of it for a count of 3 seconds, then zoom out.

8. Come back to the static Old World image – lights off, wait 1 second.

9. Lights on to show the New World like a live video, and immediately zoom right into the very middle of it as you become aware of thousands of flashes of neural pathways lighting up in the brain, and you realise that where you used to feel that sense of depression, there's a better feeling that grows stronger when you shoot your

mind forward to that memory link (step 1), imagining the time when you'll be remembering what you did today and how easily you could just Stop and Stare that Old World image.

10. Now zoom out from that New World so you're on the outside looking in.

11. Repeat steps 8–10 quickly, five more times.

12. Now zoom straight back into that New World and stay there in your mind while you drift down into the reptilian complex and into the Super Unwind – Part Two (see page 22).

13. Once back up to full awareness, explore how you feel when you think of the Old World image – if there's improvement, however slight, you're ready to move on to the next stage. If not, repeat this procedure the next day.

Text to record

The recording of this text should be played after completing steps 1–5 of the Detachment procedure, to allow you to take as much time as you need with the previous steps.

1. 'Bring the Old World image to mind and zoom right the way into it so you can imagine you're really there and even feel like you're really there for 3 seconds, then zoom out quickly so you're on the outside looking in again.' (3-second pause)

2. 'Now Stop and Stare that image to freeze it in time so that nothing is moving by even the tiniest amount and turn the light off to make it completely dark.' (5-second pause)

3. 'Turn the light on again and you can see the New World that immediately becomes live and active as you zoom right into the middle of it for a count of 3.' (3-second pause)

4. 'Now see the frozen Old World image and turn the lights off.' (Brief pause)

5. (Quickly) 'Now turn the lights on to see the New World like a live video and immediately zoom right into the very middle of it as you become aware of thousands of flashes of neural pathways lighting up in your brain, and you realise that where you used to feel that sense of depression there's a better feeling now that grows stronger when you shoot your mind forward to that memory link, imagining

the time when you'll be remembering what you did today and how easily you could just Stop and Stare that Old World image.

6.   'Now zoom out from the New World so you're on the outside looking in.'

Repeat steps 4–6 quickly, five more times.

7.   'Now zoom straight back into that New World and stay there in your mind while you drift down into the reptilian complex and into the Super Unwind – Part Two.'

Once back up to full awareness, explore how you feel when you think of the Old World image – if there's improvement, however slight, you're ready to move on to the next stage. If not, repeat this procedure the next day.

It's important that you find some noticeable uplift (however slight) from this procedure, before continuing. Also, you can choose whether or not to actually visit the location of the memory link; it's only there for your mind to be able to have a target to focus on – but if you feel you should visit it, it means that, for your particular mindset, it's likely to be a good idea.

It's important that you wait at least a week before progressing to the Energiser procedure. You might discover during this period that life seems not so much depressing as *humdrum* from time to time; this is completely normal and might feel okay – but this feeling will not last long without the Energiser.

Energiser

We're working more in the way you are used to on this one, with the New You and an Ideal Future. You already have the basis for the New You in the active video image of the New World; imagine you can see yourself in that world, fitting in perfectly with it all (and you can do this because it was you that created that New World; if you can see it, you can be it). Make this New You vivid in your mind and note where you feel that image in your body. Now for the Ideal Future: for this you need to create an image of you doing something you've always wanted to – it really doesn't matter what, as long as it is 2PF. Create a still image of whatever it is; a super high-definition photograph. It can be anything, as long as it's something you've wanted in the past but never managed to achieve – and the more you wanted it, the better (bearing in mind the 2PF concept); this is the placeholder for your Ideal Future. You've probably already got an idea of how it's going to fit into the procedure, which means that, even now, your reptilian complex is commencing and accepting the processes of change.

1. Create an image of the you that inhabits the Old World – you might discover this to be a little difficult as a result of the Detachment procedure, but that's okay. Don't worry that you're going to set yourself back in some way, since we've already guarded against that. Stop and Stare the image so that everything is totally silent and still, frozen in time.

2. Focus on the stopped image.

3. Immediately block it with the New You image.

4. Focus on the feeling of the New You in your body.

5. See thousands of flashes of neural pathways light up all over the brain from front to back and side to side and all around.

6. Dive into the placeholder of the Ideal Future as the New You, seeing yourself as if from the outside.

7. Zoom in to actually become the New You as the Ideal Future becomes active and you are on the inside looking out and feeling exactly as you want to feel, then zoom out.

8. Repeat steps 2–7 five more times, staying in the Ideal Future for 2–3 seconds longer each time.

9. Drift down into the reptilian complex and into the Super Unwind – Part Two (see page 22).

10. Once back up to full awareness, explore how the image of the Old World self feels. Ideally, there will be a sense of some disconnection, however slight – if so, you have success; the greater the disconnection, the higher the level of success.

Text to record

1. 'Find an image of the you that inhabits the Old World – even if it seems faint, or somehow a long way off, or anything else.' (5-second pause)

2. 'Stop and Stare the image so that everything is totally silent and still, and frozen in time.' (5-second pause)

3. 'Now focus on the stopped image.'

4. (Urgent and quickly from here) 'Immediately block it with the New You image.'

5. 'Now focus strongly on the feeling of the New You in your body as thousands of flashes of neural pathways light up all over your brain from front to back and side to side and all around.'

6. 'Dive into the placeholder of the Ideal Future as the New You, seeing yourself as if from the outside at first.'

7. 'Now zoom in to actually become the New You as the Ideal Future becomes active and you are on the inside looking out and feeling exactly as you want to feel and stay there for a moment.'

Repeat steps 3–7 five more times, quickly and urgently but staying at step 7 for 2–3 seconds longer each time; it's not essential to be completely accurate, as long as it is longer with every repetition.

8. 'Drift down into the reptilian complex and into the Super Unwind – Part Two.'

As usual, once back up to full awareness, explore how the image of the Old World self feels. Ideally, there will be a noticeable sense of some disconnection, however slight – if so, you have success; the greater the disconnection, the higher the level of success. This is often accompanied by a lifted sense of well-being, though if that is not present it's not an indication that the procedure has failed in any way. Quite often, the lifted sense of well-being increases day by day; where it does not, you can repeat the Energiser as often as you wish (only if there has been some form of life upheaval would you be likely to need to run the Detachment again).

In the rare circumstance where the work here proves ineffective, one of the BWRT professionals will be able to provide a therapy quite similar to that which has been covered here, though reaching far more deeply into the psyche. Alternatively, the core identity work might do the trick.

And that's what we're doing next.

Chapter 15

Complex Issues (1)

The work of this chapter and the next is the most complicated in the book, since it will allow you to work with one of the most complex of human conditions; one that's almost always stuffed to the brim with resistance to change. We're exploring the difficulties associated with core identity – that's the way you identify yourself at the deepest possible level; in other words, the basic sense of self that describes how you see yourself and how you believe others see you. It's only a problem when you really don't like who or what you are. *Who or what* might sound a little strange but the following list of unhappy core identities will probably make it easier to understand:

- 'I'm an alcoholic.'
- 'I'm a gambler.'
- 'I'm a total waste of space.'
- 'I'm just a nasty piece of work.'
- 'I'm total OCD.'
- 'I'm a bankrupt.' (which is actually quite different from 'I am bankrupt')
- 'I'm anxiety personified.' (when there is a total belief that they are naturally anxious and that it was somehow born into them)
- 'I'm a workaholic.'

As you can see from this list, it's about individuals who identify themselves as being totally just one aspect of their life. Only the last three of these are totally suitable for the work in this book (though the others can sometimes respond quite well to the material and procedures here, professional BWRT work will sort them out wonderfully). There is another common type of core identity issue that you'll read about shortly; one with which the work of this chapter can also achieve amazing results.

A core identity is only a problem if the owner of it wishes it were different. For instance, let's take the final one – 'I'm a workaholic' – and look at two extremes: we get the first possibility, where the individual is desperately miserable because their family and personal life has been wrecked as a result of their inability to stop working (which can be for a variety of reasons); the second possibility is where the individual cheerfully states they are a workaholic because they love what they do, their work includes their family and they provide a wonderful life of luxury – they still have the inability to stop working, but they enjoy every second and would probably respond with a profanity if anybody suggested they should ease up a little.

If you have a core identity with which you are happy, it's a good thing. On the other hand, if you do not have a core identity and are equally content about that, this is also a good thing. Almost everybody reading this book will, though, have a central issue in their life that affects much of what they do, one way or another, and this can easily become a core identity over a period of time.

The reason the core identity can cause a multitude of problems is simply that because it is at the core of the psyche, it affects everything the individual does. It colours their sense of self and how they believe others think of them, and therefore how they react to the world. Not only that, but the reptilian complex regards it as sacrosanct; an essential part of the personality that must be protected to ensure survival. Therefore, if any activity appears to pose a risk to it via change – including criticism, questions, even therapy – it will be guarded as vigorously as life itself. The individual concerned won't translate it that way but will be prone to some debilitating response: usually anxiety or despair. It's the same if they are required to enter into any situation where the identity is at risk in some way, even if only by some socially unacceptable behaviour being exposed to the world. The reptilian complex will protect it with whatever resource it can muster, even physical illness being a possible outcome.

Sometimes, the core identity is negatively orientated and not always immediately obvious; it is here that the work in this book can achieve amazing results, as already mentioned. In this situation, the individual will tend to feel as if they sometimes have trouble fitting in with the way the world works, or might just generally feel inadequate in some way. It's easy to establish if this situation exists in your case with three questions that you should score on a 1–10 basis (with 10 being the highest). They are two-part questions and you should only answer each after you have considered the second part – do be honest, since cheating will simply perpetuate the problem:

1. How much do you like yourself?
    - Think of something that shows that for a few moments.
2. How confident in yourself are you?
    - Visit three situations in your mind where that was important.
3. How highly do you value yourself?
    - Notice what goes on in your mind when you think about that.

When you read the results here, don't be tempted to re-evaluate. To do so will be the exact reason your life isn't exactly as you would like it to be (and it isn't, or you wouldn't be reading this book). If you deny how you really work, how will you ever fix what needs fixing? Instead, revel in the fact that you have at last discovered at least a possibility of sorting things out, once and for all. So, your score:

- **21–26:** This is (for most people) the normal range, indicating that whatever is not to your liking, it's probably not down to a core identity issue.

- **27–30:** With this score there is often a tendency toward inflexibility, though one of the indicators of this can be to deny being controlling. There may be a feeling that you must keep a grip on things because others don't. Problems can often arise in relationships.

- **20 or lower:** This is a reliable indicator of poor self-worth or inferiority complex; if the material in Chapter 7 hasn't helped a great deal, this chapter might.

The origins

The origins of the core identity, whatever that identity is, are based on confirmation of belief; it doesn't matter what that belief is, the process is always the same. Once an idea has been absorbed by the reptilian complex it will become increasingly difficult to change it and yet, at the same time, increasingly easy to confirm it – so it's a bit of a one-sided process. It's all to do with our inherited disposition to attach more importance to threat than to safety. A headline like *Hidden Disaster Looms For [your age group]* will make you read the article beneath it more avidly than *Advantage Looms*

For [your age group]. It's why a newspaper with the headline *WAR!* will sell more copies than one that says *Truce* Those ancient ancestors of ours had to be strongly attuned to threat in order to survive and so it's essentially in our genes to be more focused on downsides than upsides.

There are many ways we can gain an idea about ourselves that constitutes a threat to our integrity or our value in the world. It can come from: a groundless belief; exposure to a constant harangue about our looks, speech, intelligence, or anything else; something we overhear others saying about us; or just from an idle remark. But once the idea is taken on board, it becomes part of our existence and the reptilian complex, with its usual lack of logic, seeks to protect it as if it were vital to our survival. And it does it so well that a very strange situation soon arises; if we believe we are dim/weird/thick/ugly etc., a hundred people can tell us that we are a perfectly splendid and wonderful individual and we might politely thank them but not feel any different. But if just one person says something like 'My word, but you're dim/weird/thick/ugly' etc., we immediately think 'there – I knew it!' (or words to that effect), know immediately they're right and so strengthen the belief; such is the nature of the negative core identity. It will reject anything that conflicts with what already exists as being probably untrue and therefore potentially dangerous.

And this is why core identity issues can be so difficult to work with – or were before the advent of neuroscience-based therapies. Issues like phobias and specific anxieties are in many ways incidental to the individual's life, in that they only affect what they affect. The essential self remains the same and so, provided an effective New You and Ideal Future can be found, the threat to self is minimal or even non-existent. But a core identity issue affects everything and so we have to use a broader brush if we want to be effective. Two previous issues in this book are really core identity issues – poor self-worth and mild-to-moderate depression; though each of those can often respond to the specific therapy as shown. Where they don't though, the material here is far more likely to get a result.

No matter how the core identity problem shows itself – whether it's via alcohol, narcotics, gambling, sex obsession, or whatever – it veils the actual cause, which will be deeply embedded in the workings of the reptilian complex. It can be the result of repeated abuse, unresolved grief, deprivation, negligence, severe trauma or any one of a number of other psychological processes. Fortunately, with BWRT, we don't have to reveal that cause (though we might well find it) and so we can work in a more constructive way than digging around in memories of childhood, which has been one of the more common styles of therapy for this problem in the past.

We take an approach rather similar to when working with depression, in that we use a detachment procedure first to allow the reptilian complex enough time to recognise that the existing identity is not an essential element for survival. In this instance, it's called the Unlock procedure, which will be followed after a period of time with the Reboot procedure (the same names for the procedures used by BWRT professionals). They are based on the professional version, in fact, though they are in a greatly modified form here and obviously cannot access the depth of detail – nor the intensity – of the work a professionally trained practitioner can.

An important issue

There are several preparation concepts that must be addressed with complete honesty, since how you respond will form part of the therapeutic process itself. Before we get to them, though, there is one issue that is absolutely vital to resolve if you are not going to severely limit the success of what we are doing in this chapter (and in Chapter 16). It has already been covered in this book and it might be the case, therefore, that you have already completed the work; it is the resolution of the guilty secret (Chapter 4). In the context of what we are working on here, this refers to anything that would be embarrassing or acutely uncomfortable if others knew about it – in other words, a threat to integrity – and it is astonishingly rare for there not to be something of that sort, especially where there is a core identity issue. It might be that you cannot bear to even think about whatever it is, but that would be just another indication of how important it is to neutralise it. So, if you skipped the work in Chapter 4, go there now and set yourself free enough for the work here to be effective.

Now we'll get on to the preparation processes – they're not easy to answer and might even cause a bit of discomfort as you try, but it's only for a while and will usually be less than you might experience a lot of the time anyway. Do expect to take some time with them; the more thought you give, the better the result is likely to be.

Preparations

1. Write down how you see yourself in your mind's eye or, alternatively, how you think of yourself. Do write it down because expressing in words creates greater detail than thinking it. Be sure not to pull

punches because of embarrassment. Write it all down, however nasty you think it is – it's nothing different from what's in your head all the time anyway and you don't have to let anybody else see it.

2. This one can be a bit difficult. Write down in just a few words, or a short phrase you can remember, the worst part of what you wrote for (1). It should carry as much of the meaning as possible and needs to be something that could conceivably be changed, even if you don't think it's possible right now. *Being old*, for instance, cannot be changed but *feeling old* could. *Being me* cannot be changed, while *not liking me* can. When you have that, you can destroy the answer to (1) if you wish.

3. Now write down what you would change about that worst part, if you could (do complete this step before moving on).

4. Now, taking what you've said in (3) as a guide, describe what you would choose for yourself as your ideal self if you could just go into a shop, buy it, and put it on like a coat. This is your New Self. Don't go for second best or what you believe you can be at the moment – go for what you really want. All that's important is the 2PF concept: it must be possible for somebody to do it, it must be plausible for you to do it, and it must be fair (in other words, it must be just for you and not to spite anybody else). Think how you would look if you were already that ideal self, looking from the outside in – and make it vivid; it doesn't matter if you can't actually feel it at the moment. The self-image is an inextricable part of the problems of your old self, and that problem doesn't exist in the New Self.

5. Whenever anybody is trying to make a change for themselves, there's almost always somebody who would like to prevent that change for whatever reason; often because they fear losing control or have a perceived superior position. You can either not mention anything about it and just wait to see if they notice – they should – or you can be ready with a response to whatever negativity they might come up with (which would often be along the lines of 'I liked you more before you created change for yourself'). Here are some potential responses:

    a. 'Really? Why do you say that?'

    b. 'Sorry – I don't agree with you.'

    c. 'Okay – but why are you trying to stop me?'

    d. 'Thank you!'

e.   'Sorry you feel like that. I like the way I'm changing though.'

f.   'Really? I hadn't noticed that. Oh well, never mind.'

g.   'How on earth did you arrive at that conclusion?'

h.   'And your point is?'

Don't worry about hurting someone's feelings – after all, they're trying to do just that to you. And if they get angry, it'll be because they didn't get their own way, which pretty much proves the point. Always remember that whatever anybody says about you, they're talking about themselves, not you – it's just their opinion. And that's the cue for another possible response that would be entirely accurate: 'That's what you think.'

6.   Finally, write down what will be the very best thing about being that New You – don't just think it, write it down in detail. Remember, expressing something in words is far more powerful than just thinking it, and seeing it in your mind's eye is much easier when you've written it down. Make it a vivid description.

These six preparations are an essential part of the success of what you are doing here, so do be thorough. Though written in a style suitable for self-help, they are based on some of the questions that BWRT professionals use when they're working with core identity issues; they activate certain neural pathways in the reptilian complex to make change far more readily available than otherwise.

A checklist

To finish this chapter, we're going to run through a checklist to make sure everything is as good as it can get at this stage before moving on to the two procedures that will create your brand-new way of being.

The first thing to check is whether there have been any previously unrecognised issues, problems or uncomfortable situations that have come to light as a result of your thoughts and ponderings as you worked through those preparations. It can be a realisation of a difficulty or an anxiety that wasn't clear before; if there is anything, do work at it with one of the other procedures in this book before continuing here. The core identity work needs as little resistance as possible. Also, remember you cannot change anybody else – all you can do is change your response to whatever it is that you find to be a problem.

The second thing is to make sure there's not some psychological benefit to you in hanging onto the old self. This is not at all uncommon and can be that you have an excuse for failure or not participating in some things, for example, or you like the attention and care you get from others as a result of, for instance, low self-worth or relationships repeatedly failing. It might be that you believe that you are the way you are as a result of something that somebody did (or didn't do) when you were growing up and you're resentful at letting them off by getting better. Remember the important advice from Chapter 6: it doesn't matter who did what to you, or when, nor how often they repeated it; the only person who can sort it out is you. You're not giving in – you're stopping them from being in control of what you do and do not do in life.

The third thing is just to check that you're not unnecessarily concerned about what others will think about the changes you are making. Whatever changes we make for ourselves, the lives of other people might be affected – but if you have followed the 2PF rule in your plans, there is no reason you should modify them to suit the needs of others. This quote has been attributed to at least two different people,[1] but whoever said it knew a thing or two:

> 'Be who you are and say how you feel, because those who matter won't mind, and those who mind don't matter.'

The fourth and final element is a check to see that you have been completely honest with yourself throughout the work of this chapter. This is possibly one of the most important aspects, since any unfinished business, or anything dismissive like 'but that wasn't really important' is just another connecting thread to the old you.

And if there's something causing you a problem that you really cannot sort out on your own, then there's a BWRT professional practitioner waiting to help you. Details of how to find one are on page 178, but for the moment we will assume that all is well and move on to the active part of dealing with your core identity.

---

1   See https://quoteinvestigator.com/2012/12/04/those-who-mind/#note-4956-1.

Chapter 16

Complex Issues (2)

The procedures you're going to discover in this chapter are necessarily more complicated than those covered previously and it's important to ensure the success of the first one – the Unlock – before moving on to the Reboot a week or so later. There is a daily exercise to perform during the week between the two, and this will (a) sustain the energy in the new neural pathways that have been created, and (b) prepare the reptilian complex to embrace the processes of the New You (the New Self from the last chapter).

Before we get to the meat of the work, we're going to engage in a little thought experiment – along with some other preparation work. From the outside looking in, imagine a few seconds (maybe half a minute or so) of a situation from the past two or three years, where life has been difficult or even downright disastrous. There's no need to recapture the feeling of the event or circumstance, though it's fine if this happens naturally. Now imagine that same situation, still from the outside looking in, but this time with the New You handling it; imagine how you would explain to a therapist the difference between the two scenes. There's no need to write it down this time, though it can be beneficial to speak it aloud (this is optional) as you observe the scene unfold. It doesn't matter if you can't actually feel the difference at this stage, and it also doesn't mean everything is sorted if you can – there's a fair bit to do yet to lock everything in place. When the scene you have recalled is finished, repeat the exercise with two more different situations. If you have been able to observe and explain the difference between then and now, however slight and whether or not you actually feel different as you look at both versions, it is a good indicator that everything is going at least as well as it needs to at this stage.

Now for some preparation, as usual. First, recall the image of your old self, as if from the outside, and get the PAL. The original feeling associated with the old self might have faded a little since the first time you created it in the last chapter. This being the case, score it as if you knew it was going to come back later in full force and never change – as if this were how you would be for the rest of your life, along with all the associated baggage and issues that you know so well. Don't worry if the feeling of that old self comes flooding back; this is of no consequence and might even strengthen the work you are about to do. We'll call this the *bad* PAL. Now bring the New You image to mind and again get the PAL – this time, though, it's a *good* PAL and it needs to be at least as high as that of the old self; ideally a bit higher so that the New You effectively cancels out the old self. Of course, if they are both at 10, that's as good as it gets. So, here we have two PALs – a good one and a bad one.

The Unlock

For both the Unlock and Reboot procedures, recording and following with your eyes closed from step 3 is essential. It might seem to be a laborious exercise but, as previously mentioned, it really is the way to get something that is as close to a session or two with a professional practitioner as it's possible to get with self-help.

1. We don't need an Ideal Future for this part of the work, though we will be creating one in the Reboot. We do still need a future link to act as a focal point for the reptilian complex though, and the simplest way to create one is to imagine an image of you preparing for the Reboot next week. Do that now.

2. Now you need a few seconds of mental video (or a thought sequence if you find the mental video difficult), as if from the outside looking in at the New You in some totally ordinary everyday situation and feeling good; strolling through a park, making a cup of tea, sitting watching TV, gardening, shopping – any minor, benign or even boring activity that is not in any way connected with the reason you're working with this core identity issue. To ensure enough clarity, write down the storyline similar to this example: *Grassy park, sunny, me looking super-confident; wearing jeans, a top and trainers; carrying a bottle of water, walking near trees by a large pond; smiling at somebody walking a dog.* You'll play the imagined scene in a continuous loop in the procedure. Create that now.

3. With eyes closed, bring the image of your old self to mind. Zoom in to the very worst part of it to focus fully on the worst feeling. When

it's as bad as it can get or as you can stand, immediately Stop and Stare it to lock it in its own time.

4. Focus on the locked memory and then immediately onto your mental video.

5. Imagine thousands of flashes of neural pathways lighting up in each part of the brain as you relay the mental video to the front, back, left side, right side, whole brain as you count to five.

6. Watch that mental video speeding up a little and as you get to the end of it, shoot your mind forward to that future memory link of you preparing to start the Reboot next week.

7. Repeat steps 4–6 as quickly as you can.

8. Now do the Super Unwind – Part Two (see page 22).

9. Test the bad PAL – it's possible that you might have trouble finding the image, or it will be very faint. Now test the good PAL; ideally this will be at least as high as it was to start with, or even higher.

Text to record

Be sure to complete steps 1 and 2 of the Unlock before closing your eyes and listening to this recording:

1. 'Find the image of the old self in your mind and zoom in to the very worst part of it and make it as bad as you can get or as bad as you can stand.' (5-second pause)

2. 'Now Stop and Stare the image to stop it and freeze it in its own time.'

3. 'Focus on that locked memory, then immediately onto your mental video instead.'

4. 'And now imagine thousands of flashes of neural pathways lighting up in each part of your brain as you relay the mental video to the front, back, left side, right side, whole brain as you count to five.' (5-second pause)

5. 'You can see the mental video speeding up a little and as you get to the end of it shoot your mind forward to that future memory link of you preparing to start the Reboot next week.'

Repeat steps 3–5, speaking as quickly and urgently as you can.

6. 'Now do the Super Unwind – Part Two.'

Once you've completed the Super Unwind, immediately test the bad PAL – it's possible that you might even have trouble finding the image, or it will be very faint. Now test the good PAL; ideally this will be at least as high as it was to start with, or even higher.

If the bad PAL can still be triggered to its original level, there's almost certainly a reason to hang on to the old self (whether you can identify it or not). Occasionally, somebody might believe it's because the brain has obviously recognised it would not be good for them to change – but this is not likely to be the truth. It's far more probable that there is an unadmitted benefit to keeping the old self, or some uncomfortable issue or situation associated with the New You; maybe there will be an added responsibility that you don't want to take on, or the need to finally deal with something you've been avoiding like the plague. If you can't find the reason, this procedure is not going to work for you as it stands. You have three choices:

- Go back to the beginning of Chapter 15 and work through everything again with total honesty.
- Seek the help of a Registered Advanced BWRT Practitioner, who will know how to deal with it (details in Chapter 18).
- Work on any aspects of yourself with the material in the other chapters of this book – this can sometimes loosen stubborn blocks.

Consolidation break

You've already read that we work with the Unlock to allow the reptilian complex to recognise that the old self is not an essential element of survival, but there are two further reasons. The first is that the core identity has been damped down and may not even be noticeable after the Unlock; this means the reptilian complex needs some time to adjust to the different feedback from conscious thought processes – and it will be different; it might even be hugely noticeable. The Reboot is designed to complete and consolidate the changes before the old self attempts to reassert itself, so it is important that the interval between the two is around seven-to-ten days. Earlier or later than this can still work perfectly well, but the experience of professional therapists suggests the optimum gap is a week – the period to which many therapists work. This is not surprising, since the vast part of all people's lives are governed by a weekly procedure, and so the reptilian complex responds well to it. Also, the daily exercise you will be doing during this week will become steadily more familiar so that, by the end, the newness has faded somewhat and a secure foundation to support the New You has been created.

The daily exercise

Do this exercise at least once every day – ideally twice or even three times (which you would be required to do if working with a BWRT practitioner). It's not difficult and is based around the Super Unwind – Part One (see page 21). Once you have got down into that reptilian complex, bring the locked image of the old self to mind. Hold it for a few moments before imagining the feeling and image of the New You enveloping you and filling every pore of your body. Hold it for a count of 10 seconds – no rushing – then repeat it from the locked image another two or three times, finishing with the feeling of the New You all around you, or even feeling as if it's actually radiating out from you. It might be the case that you start to have some difficulty seeing or focusing on the locked image of the old self and that's okay – just search for it for a moment or two anyway and, as it becomes evident that it's not available, go to the New You.

After you've finished the exercise, immediately make a note of the time of day and give the process a score between 1 and 10, where 1 means it was difficult and 10 means it was very easy. Finally, just once each day, write a brief description – up to ten words – of how you feel about your New Self. Ideally, this will be done after the first Super Unwind session but must be written once a day, even if it's the same as the previous day. As before, don't be tempted to just think these events – be sure to actually do them exactly as they are described here – and if you find yourself thinking any of the following, be aware that you might well be looking at part of the reason for many of the difficulties in your life.

- 'I don't have time.'
- 'I can't be bothered.'
- 'It's too complicated.'
- 'I feel stupid doing it.'
- 'I don't see how it can help.'
- 'It's boring.'

The scores you give each day should increase as you become more used to the exercise (unless they're at the top from the very start) and the only bad news would be if they reduced over the week; this would indicate doubt of some sort and the advice would be the same as that given at the end of the Unlock.

The Reboot

So here you are, one week or so on from completing the Unlock, and the chances are you're feeling pretty good about yourself. Don't be fooled into thinking it's all done and dusted now or all over bar the shouting. It often feels like that at this stage, but those new neural pathways are still fragile and need a little more work to strengthen and set them securely.

There's also one other thing to think about: a situation or any individual likely to sabotage your success. For instance, if you were intent on becoming a non-smoker ('I'm a smoker' is sometimes a core identity, after all) and you had to regularly be in an environment where others smoked, that would possibly be a vulnerable situation; as would somebody trying to tempt you with such remarks as 'Oh go on, have one. One's not going to do you any harm.' If there's anything like that around you, you will probably have become aware of it by now. There's a simple *trigger guard* procedure we can use which will tend to reduce the risk of such events having any effect. Like one or two other processes, it's a broad-brush procedure that will cover most circumstances (though not necessarily every single thing that could exist, because that would probably take an entire book). There's no great preparation needed here, since it's based on the Virtual Reality process used in many other parts of the book:

Trigger Guard

1. Imagine the vulnerable situation and make it as vivid as you can.

2. Stop and Stare the image so that it becomes locked in time and immediately starts to fade.

3. See yourself as the New You, staring at the image as it fades a little more.

4. See yourself turning and striding away with an air of total confidence.

5. Dive into the scene to actually become the New You, with a satisfied feeling in your body of leaving the problem even further behind.

6. A congratulatory flash of thousands of neural pathways fills your brain for a moment, then rushes through your body for a count of three.

7. Repeat steps 3–6 five times quickly.

8. Pause for a count of 10 while you relocate yourself to now, then open your eyes.

Text to record

1. 'Make the vulnerable situation really vivid in your mind.' (5-second pause)

2. 'Stop and Stare it to freeze it in time and notice that it starts to fade.' (5-second pause)

3. 'Now see the New You, staring at that frozen image as it fades a bit more.'

4. (Urgent and quickly now) 'See yourself turning and striding away looking totally confident then dive straight into the scene to actually become the New You with a satisfied feeling in your body of leaving the problem even further behind you.'

5. 'A flash of thousands of neural pathways fills your brain for a moment, then it's as if it rushes through your body as you count to three. (3-second pause)

Repeat steps 3–5 five times quickly.

6. 'Now pause for a slow count of ten while you bring yourself back to now where you are right at this minute, then open your eyes.'

The procedure

All the preparation is now done and so you're ready to start on the Reboot itself. It's not a quick and easy method by any means, since we're working with a complicated and multifaceted situation which has to be thorough. As a result, the procedure itself is the most complicated one in the book – but it is also the most powerful. There's one preparation needed: you'll be focusing on your old self involved in the behaviour or circumstance that causes the problem and you should choose the worst one you can remember, even if you seem to have no feeling associated with it any more (the Unlock might have defused it). It is perfectly permissible to choose a different situation, as long as it involves the same problem. As before, this one really must be recorded and listened to from step 3 onwards.

1. Create another few seconds of a mental video (or thought sequence) as you did for the Unlock, but this time of the best thing about being the New You – the preparation for which you did in Chapter 15

(preparation (6) on page 151). Again, write it out so that you know exactly what it shows because you'll be playing this in a loop throughout the active part of the procedure. Be sure that it illustrates everything that is the New You and make it absolutely focused on you, looking evidently as if you're feeling the way you want to feel. It must be vibrant and alive.

2. Now think of some situation in the near future where your old self would have been suffering – ideally, this will be a genuine event but invention and imagination is okay if there's nothing that comes to mind. Create a strong image of being on the outside looking in, where you can see the back of you watching the scene – this is the placeholder for your Ideal Future. At one point you'll be switching from your mental video to the Ideal Future and back again; so the mental video (or thought sequence) is the way you are, while the Ideal Future is something you will be doing.

3. Bring the image of the old self to mind, looking at it as if from the outside, and make sure it is dynamically active and as vivid as you can see it or think it. Hold the image or thought in your mind, as if viewing a hugely detailed memory for a few seconds, and then Stop and Stare the very worst part of it so that it is completely locked in time forever; so that it's just a shell with no meaning any more. And now do the next part as quickly as you can with a feeling of it being urgent.

4. See your old self just walking away from that shell of a memory and leaving all that behind and with every step you see the magical transformation into the New You taking place as you fully adopt this wonderful new version of you and you can feel the excitement coursing through every neuron in your brain and in every fibre and cell of your entire body as you become the you that you were always designed to be. And zoom in now to actually become that fantastic new self, so that it's just as if you're looking out through your eyes at the world around you.

5. And now start that mental video rolling; make it as vivid and real and as vibrant as you can so that every single one of those neural pathways in your brain are actively carrying that image right into the front, the back, the left side, the right side and then the whole of your brain as you count from one to five – front, back, side, side, whole brain.

6. And feel it filling your entire self as you jump forward to that Ideal Future and dive right into that placeholder so it's as if you are

actually there just long enough to feel the fantastic New You enjoying every second of being alive, before you hurtle back to that locked shell to check it out and notice that it's somehow fading into the past, becoming fainter each time you look at it.

7. Repeat steps 4–6 five times.

8. Dive into the Ideal Future and stay there for as long as you want.

9. Continue into the Super Unwind – Part Two (see page 22).

10. Once back to full awareness, explore both PALs – the best possible result is that the good one is at 10 and the bad one is at 1 or 0, or even so absent that you are not able to score it.

Text to record

As with the Unlock, be sure to complete steps 1 and 2 of the Reboot thoroughly before listening to the following recording:

1. 'Bring the image of the old self to mind, looking at it as if from the outside and make it as realistically active and vivid as you can. Study that old self for a few seconds and then Stop and Stare the very worst part of it to lock it in its own time forever so that it's just a shell with no meaning. Only you can move out of that shell and the rest is locked forever.' (5-second pause)

2. (Quickly and urgently) 'And now see your old self just walking away from that shell of a memory and leaving all that stuff behind, and with every step you see a magical transformation into the New You happening, and as you fully adopt this wonderful new version of you, you feel the excitement flowing through every neuron in your brain and every fibre and cell of your entire body as you realise you are becoming the person you were always designed to be. Zoom in now to actually become that fantastic new self so it's as if you're looking out through your eyes at the world around you.' (5-second pause)

3. 'Now start that mental video rolling; make it as vivid and real and as vibrant as you can so that every single one of those neural pathways in your brain is actively carrying that image right into the front, the back, the left side, the right side and then the whole of your brain as you count from one to five – front, back, side, side, whole brain.' (5-second pause)

4. 'And feel it filling your entire self now as you jump forward to that Ideal Future and dive right into that placeholder so it's as if you are

actually there just long enough to feel the fantastic New You enjoying every second of being alive before you hurtle back to that locked shell to check it out and notice that it's somehow fading into the past, becoming fainter each time you look at it.' (No pause – continue immediately)

Repeat steps 2–4 five times.

5.   Now, 'Dive into the Ideal Future and stay there for as long as you want, then continue into the Super Unwind – Part Two.'

Once back to full awareness, explore both PALs – the best possible result is that the good PAL is at 10 and the bad one is at 1 or 0, or even so absent that you are not able to score it. This is a longer procedure than most of the others in the book because it has a serious task to complete; it's setting you free from what used to be and encouraging your reptilian complex to absorb everything you need to have a life that works for you as you want it. Dismiss any idea that this is not possible – that part of your brain will link everything you've worked at to you and your general way of being, just as it has for thousands of people in professional sessions.

It's extremely rare for core identity work not to make any change but should you feel that this is the case, it suggests that there might be some unrecog-nised deeper issue that is outside the scope of this book. There's more about this situation, and some guidance on dealing with it, in Chapter 18.

Conclusions

If all has gone well, it's likely that you'll very soon start to feel as if not much change has happened. This is because, when they work at their very best, the procedures covered in these last two chapters restore the self that biology intended you to be – so it feels completely normal and not at all remarkable. The fact remains that whatever you were working on now gives you far less of a problem than it used to, though even that sometimes gets dismissed with 'Well, I don't think I was actually that bad', or 'Well, nothing remarkable happened – it wasn't anything to do with the book. I just decided to make some changes and got on with it, that's all.'

And of course, you did – but maybe that was because you'd been reading this book.

Chapter 17

Planning for a Great Future

Strictly speaking, this chapter is not directly associated with BWRT but is about personality types – as mentioned in Chapter 10 and discussed in the book, *Warriors, Settlers & Nomads*,[1] which sits on the bookshelves of many therapists; they love it for the ease with which it allows an understanding of what makes any individual tick – and it is for that reason it is referred to here. Now you've resolved all sorts of issues, you can more easily apply your natural strengths and resources to your future to find the best life you can.

The origins of each type are based in evolutionary history, though that alone would take an entire chapter (and more) to explore, so is not covered here. Suffice to say that from the beginnings of civilisation the different tribes (warlike types, community-minded groups and those who had never stayed in one place for longer than they had to) began to interbreed so that, many hundreds of generations later, the modern human has inherited something of all three main personality styles. There's usually one that dominates when push comes to shove, though we can access the resources of all three types to a varying degree. Where there isn't a dominant process, the Combination personality comes into play (which brings its own strengths and weaknesses, of course). There actually isn't a better or best personality type – each has its own advantages and disadvantages – and the two main benefits you can gain from learning about them are:

- Recognising how others behave and how to get the best from interactions.

- A full understanding of self and how best to handle life in general.

---

1   Watts, T. *Warriors, Settlers & Nomads*.

Who are you?

There are four descriptions here that are rather more detailed than those given earlier (see page 98) (though still only really give a potted view) and although a personality test can be used, it is also easy enough to identify yourself by reading about the way each one works. Here are the descriptions – and don't be tempted to ignore the negatives, since they often reveal the real you – and that of your friends, family and workmates.

Warrior

This is someone who likes to be in control of their life and, as far as possible, of the world around them, since they hate having to be answerable to others and are certainly not very good at being told what to do (though they are usually good at organising others and telling them what to do).

They are not big on displays of softness and affection as a rule, though they might well tend to feel more than they show, and they are usually immensely loyal to their friends and allies. Not flashy in their dress or speech, they often answer a question with another question and give little away by their face expression or body language. Good in a crisis, this is the one you can rely on in any emergency.

Positives: forthright, direct, tenacious, organised, sensible, observant, thorough.

Negatives: critical, irritable, contrary, combative, judgemental, sometimes manipulative, hates being seen to be wrong.

Based on: the need to be in control.

Settler

The Settler usually has an urge to look after everything living – be it human or beast, ugly or beautiful – and makes little distinction, if any, between them. They are the least judgemental of individuals and will usually help even those who have previously wronged them if they are in real trouble.

This is a sometimes complicated individual who tries hard to see the best in others – and often manages it where most fail. By nature loving and affectionate, they can react with visible hurt to unkindness or any form of dismissal and can occasionally be rather naive about the true intentions of others. Conservative in their dress and manner, they are able to show their feelings and responses to most situations, albeit conservatively.

Positives: kind, sympathetic, friendly, supportive, agreeable, nurturing, calm.

Negatives: can sulk better than most, easily upset, moody, goes silent but won't say why, depressive, self-punishing, doormat syndrome.

Based on: the need to be loved and nurtured.

Nomad

The Nomad loves to tell stories and it can be difficult to know whether what they are saying is true or exaggerated for effect – and they will sometimes act out an event with much expression, body movement and expletives. These are almost always highly expressive individuals who use colourful language and lots of laughter and/or noise.

The Nomad loves to be the centre of attention, likes to shock and wants to be top at everything – though without having to work to get there – and they sometimes make it by sheer dint of personality and outlandish claims. Usually showy or untidy dressers, they like to be different from the crowd and can be relied upon to liven up gatherings and haul somebody out of the deepest gloom within moments.

Positives: enthusiastic, energetic, excitable, dramatic, inventive, charismatic, charming.

Negatives: can be shallow, lies easily, sometimes irresponsible, fickle, self-indulgent, profane, impatient.

Based on: the need for admiration and recognition.

Combination

Where this is high energy, they are natural achievers and often have a wide range of skills at professional level – but the lower that energy is, the more they tend towards the jack of all trades and the master bodger.

The Combination personality is difficult to get to know, since their thought processes and conversation are different from the crowd. With a high intrinsic energy they can be exhaustingly intense, while at the other end of the scale they might be downright boring. It's not easy to spot a combination personality by dress or demeanour, since there is not usually anything specifically distinctive. But now you know, you'll spot one when you see one.

Positives: any of those listed above, but with a leaning towards Nomad.

Negatives: any of those listed above but with a strong leaning towards Warrior.

Based on: the need to do their own thing.

Now what?

So, you've decided who you (probably) are and identified friends, family, workmates and a few film stars and politicians to boot; now you're wondering what else you can do with this amazing new information. Well, quite a lot as it happens. The first thing to do is make the resources of each instantly available when you need them and the easiest way to do this is by creating a vivid mental image (VMI) of each persona. This ideally will be a persona from times past, not a modern individual; if you choose somebody you know, you will start trying to behave like them – and that's not the purpose of the exercise. Here are some ideas to inspire you, though you don't have to choose from them:

Warriors: Celtic kings and chieftains, warrior queens, Normans, Vikings, crusaders, knights, Native Americans, samurai, Zulus, shoguns, Trojans, Nubian kings or queens, Roman gladiators and centurions, Chinese and Japanese emperors, ancient Huns, Saxons.

Settlers: homesteaders, ancient farmers, livestock workers, ancient builders, carers of all descriptions, healers, craftsmen of all types, teachers, monks, nuns, clothiers and dressmakers, barbers, shopkeepers, researchers, philosophers, artists, musicians, composers and *searchers for truth*.

Nomads: gypsies, wandering minstrels, tinkers, ancient Arabs, actors, tricksters, travellers, sorcerers, witches, warlocks, wizards, itinerant musicians, soothsayers, prophets and seers, thieves and pickpockets, highwaymen, court jesters, storytellers, outlaws, pirates, dancers, magicians, conjurors, illusionists.

Choose one of each that appeals to you – it doesn't matter why – and spend some time imagining what they would be like; how they look, sound, move and show their special resource. They can have a name or just be

Warrior, Settler or Nomad. So, you might have a Nomad wizard with twinkling eyes, a long white beard and a chuckle in his voice; he moves as if he's floating just above the ground, holding a glowing orb from which all his magical powers emanate. Or maybe a Warrior queen with steely grey eyes, strength in her voice and an unwavering gaze from a beautiful face that belies her determination and resolve; she sits astride an armoured horse and holds a crossbow at the ready. And perhaps the Settler is an asexual musician who seems to radiate kindness from an angelic face, has a smooth and quiet voice and sits on a long couch playing a lyre – or perhaps a triangle that they strike to tell you they're with you.

You get the idea; use your imagination to its limit to create VMIs that really work for you so that, as you think of each one, you automatically find yourself thinking of (and feeling) their strengths and resources. It's important to recognise that, since you created them, they really do represent those resources and strengths in your psyche. Take your time with each one. To get the best out of the exercise, complete the Super Unwind – Part One (see page 21) before creating each image – this can greatly enhance your imaginative powers. You don't have to create them all on the same day, though if you have enough time (with a 15-minute break between them) it can be a great way to work.

Now the test

Okay, now it's time to see how effective your VMIs are – and if one turns out to be lacking, that's not a problem; you will just go through the creation process for that one again. In the rare event none of them seem to do very much for you, it might be that you need to suspend disbelief for a little while when you create them and recognise, too, that they are simply visual labels to remind you of totally natural parts of your own thought processes. We've not created anything new in your mind, other than the VMIs – the processes were already there, or you would not have understood them when you read about them.

Now, think of some situation that you find a little difficult to deal with. It can be anything; returning faulty goods to a shop, complaining about a meal in a restaurant, saying no to a request, somebody cutting you up when driving, somebody wrongly (and rudely) accusing you of something – anything that feels uncomfortable. Make it vivid enough that you can actually feel that discomfort. Now bring your Warrior to mind and focus, for a moment or two, on the sound of them and whatever the symbol of their strength is. Then vividly imagine yourself actually in that situation, noticing how it feels. Do the same thing with the Settler, and then with the Nomad. Notice which one has the best response to deal with the situation. Is it the Warrior, steadfastly standing their ground; the Settler with their reasonable negotiating skills; or the Nomad, charming the problem out of existence? The image that worked best for you is the one to use next time you are in that situation, of course; or maybe you'll have two – or even all three – in your mind when you need them.

It might be that you had to search a little to find the response in this imaginary situation (though some people find an instant recognition) but it gets stronger every time you use it, just as any skill does – and this is a skill that huge numbers of people use on a daily basis. After a while, you'll be able to instantly access whichever VMI(s) you need without any deliberation – and the real test, of course, will be the next time you find yourself in any uncomfortable situation. The VMI can be in your mind in an instant and your responses will be so totally natural that it will not feel at all remarkable. It's even likely, as stated at the end of the previous chapter, that you will want to deny that it had anything at all to do with what you've been reading here – and if so, that's the best fix you could ever have.

Decisions, decisions

Everybody experiences the total inability to make a decision from time to time, and it can be for a number of reasons:

- More than one choice; all bad, but one must be made.
- More than one choice; all good, but only one can be made.
- Something has to be left out of several possibilities.
- What you really want is not the most sensible.
- What you really want is not available.
- What you want is different from what somebody else says you should have.
- Somebody else already has what you want and you don't want to copy them.

Although it might sound a bit strange at first, when a decision is difficult it's often because there's disagreement between your VMIs. It's actually not as daft as it might sound; almost everybody has had the experience where they want to buy something new, but don't want to spend the money – that's often a disagreement between the Nomad part of you (Nomads love new things) and the Warrior (Warriors like to hang on to their resources; money, in this case). Perhaps you fancy a razzy new outfit but you worry what people might think; well, that's the Nomad again (who loves razzy) disagreeing with the Settler (the community-minded, conservative one). Or maybe someone is trying to put you in your place and you don't feel able to say anything, but also think you should – you can probably work out that's the Warrior and Settler at odds with each other.

It's usually quite easy to resolve the impasse; just find out what the other VMI (you can consider them parts of you, if you prefer it – many do) thinks about the situation. Take that first example (where you want to buy something but don't want to spend the money) – the Settler will lend weight one way or the other, depending on the importance of the product. Or in that last situation between the Settler and the Warrior, the Nomad would either have a quick retort or decide it just wasn't worth the bother. When it's two against one, you can usually feel the decision being made. Of course, whatever decision you make cannot possibly please everybody (real-life everybody that is, not the VMIs) but all you can do is make up your mind as to what's best for you – ultimately, that's always the best decision and the one you are most likely to be happy with in the long term.

There are actually many more uses for the Warriors, Settlers & Nomads (WSN) concept. With practice, you can begin to recognise somebody's probable type within a few seconds of meeting them (though this skill takes a little time to acquire). You can make complex major decisions by considering how each VMI/part feels about what the other two prefer, and you can often reduce internal conflict by reining in or boosting the qualities of the other two; for instance, the Settler-based individuals are often uncomfortable with having a lot of money and might experience feelings of guilt, which can be eased if the Nomad in you decides not to be ostentatious with it and the Warrior in you decides to use it wisely, rather than just splashing it around all over the place. You can even learn to switch modes in an instant to get the best out of any situation where you want to gain advantage. And it should go without saying that you can operate in any mode you like for given situations – always Warrior, for instance, in situations where you need to keep control (such as business management).

The New You

Probably one of the best things you can do with this new skill is to discover which of the three will be best to strengthen the New You you have created as a result of the different procedures you have used in this book. It's not at all unusual to discover that in spite of the fact you might have used four or five – or more – of those procedures, the New You in each case is remark-ably similar to the others. And now that you've discovered the best version of you for the situations you were working with, you will be able to hone them to near-perfection when you bring the WSN concept to bear. In fact, when you look at all of them, you can easily work out the largest VMI pres-ence overall and create a universal New You who can deal with anything the world throws at you.

And that really can get you the best life possible.

Chapter 18

A Daily Plan and Professional Help

In this final chapter, we're going to have a look at how you can devise a daily and weekly plan to help you maintain what you've created. We'll also consider what the professional BWRT practitioner can do that this book couldn't. We'll have a look at the two main reasons for this – and how the professional therapist works – later, but we'll start with the design of a daily and weekly procedure.

It's not something you have to do (for the most part, the changes you have made for yourself with the procedures in this book are here to stay), but a daily mental workout and a weekly *check it and refresh it* session can keep you on top form; even on those occasions where life has become a bit trying, or where the universe plays one of its cosmic jokes. It's not hugely different to the athlete training regularly or the musician practising every day – it's to keep all the associated neural pathways in that reptilian complex working as effortlessly and perfectly as they can; it's about keeping ahead of the game. So, let's get straight to it.

Day start

A good way to begin the day – maybe even before you've even got out of bed – is to get the reptilian complex prepared for whatever the next few hours are going to bring. Once you're used to it, it will probably take only a couple of minutes. You can easily adjust it as necessary, depending on what the day ahead might bring. You can run it like the Virtual Reality process that you've already practised several times on your journey through the work of this book. We're not seeking to solve a problem this time, so the first task is to create the image of you that is perfect for the day ahead; you can create it fresh each time, based on one or other of your WSN VMIs, or have a standard version (clearly brimming with energy and confidence, for example) that you use every time. You might, of course, want a more laid-back version for holidays and for when there's nothing important happening that day. The choice is yours. We'll call this image the Day Self.

We're going to use a version of the very first exercise you did in Chapter 1, since it's easy to remember (though you can record it if you prefer) and is perfect for this job. It's a good idea to set a timer for 5 minutes if you're using this procedure first thing in the morning, in case you doze off again (it's not uncommon, especially if you're a little sleep deprived). If this happens, do it a second time as best you can with your eyes open.

1. Create or bring to mind the Day Self for that day.

2. Imagine a clock with an hour hand, a minute hand and a hand that counts the seconds; so you can see the clock is working.

3. See yourself exactly as you are at this very moment – lying in bed, for example. See it as if from the outside looking in and make it as realistic as you can.

4. Stop and Stare the clock and see that everything is locked in time, except you.

5. See yourself getting up from where you are and taking five fast steps out of that scene, with each step morphing into the Day Self.

6. Zoom in to actually become that Day Self and see the clock jump forward to catch up with now as you count five more fast steps, feeling the very essence of the Day Self filling your mind and body.

7. Repeat steps 3–6 four or five more times or until you feel ready to go.

Each step doesn't have to be clearly separated from the one before it and, after a little practice, it's likely that the process will begin to feel just like a Virtual Reality video.

Super Unwind

Always a good thing to do once a day – if you're pressed for time, just Part One (see page 21) can do great things for your sense of well-being. Do make sure you're unlikely to be disturbed, though, whether you're doing the whole procedure or just Part One or Part Two (you can use either separately, just as you wish). It's extraordinarily irritating to be hauled out of your contemplation of the universe, or your deepest self, by your mobile phone alert – or somebody enquiring if you'd like a cup of tea.

Day end

Last thing at night, let your mind drift through the events of the day; if everything is either good or unremarkable, go straight into the Super Unwind – Part One (see page 21) for as long as you wish – and if you're already in bed, continue into Part Two for a great night's sleep.

If you find yourself revisiting an event or situation where you were uncomfortable, check to see which of the VMIs was most active; then run it twice more, with each of the others active in turn. If you notice it felt better with one of the others, just mentally accept it and go straight into both parts of the Super Unwind to consolidate the changes. Your reptilian complex will activate the relevant neural pathways so that if you encounter a similar situation in the future, you'll find yourself feeling and reacting differently.

The weekly plan

It's best to choose a specific time and day to do this procedure every week – if you leave it open-ended it will be at different times (and sometimes forgotten altogether), which is not a good way to program the reptilian complex.

If you want to look after your body as well as your mind, then the procedure in Chapter 5 – the Immune Booster – is a must. It's most effective to do the whole thing (it takes only a few minutes when you're used to it) but if you're really pressed for time, this mini version is an option:

Mini Immune Boost

1. Breathe in and hold.
2. Fingertips on thymus with awareness of fingers and body then send thoughts to:
   - Nerve paths to thymus.
   - Nerve path down spine to the first adrenal.
   - Nerve path down spine to the second adrenal.
3. Breathe out, remove your fingertips and then replace them quickly.
4. Repeat steps 1–3 several times.

You can do this with your eyes open or closed; if you're very clever you can even do it while you're on the move (not while driving, though). Other than this reinforcement of your immune system, it's a good idea to check how your psyche is responding to any other processes you've worked on – you might need to run them two or three times on a weekly basis to retain effectiveness, but they will gain energy every time and eventually the problem will become an ex-problem. It's not unusual to discover that something you've worked on was actually hiding a lesser issue, which begins to seem more important after the more uncomfortable stuff has been dealt with – but, of course, you know exactly what to do about that now. And if there's no specific procedure in the book for it, then the basic one in Chapter 3 is an excellent fallback process which will (at the very least) make a dent in anything you address with it.

And now it's time to have a look at how the professionals can help you when you need it.

The professionals

There are two main reasons why a professional BWRT practitioner might be able to help you where the material in this book didn't. Self-help can never be as effective as a professional therapist, for the reasons mentioned in the Introduction. In addition, the professional therapist receives a training in methodologies that cannot be used on oneself, needing a delivery *from the outside* as it were. Also, they have a whole library of specialised interventions and they know how to use them to effortlessly guide your mind past any tendency to hang on to the problem.

It's important to understand that every BWRT professional practitioner is already a professional therapist before they even start on their BWRT training – and many of them are psychologists or psychiatrists – so when you consult with anybody you find on the BWRT Professionals website[1] you can rest assured that you are in good hands with somebody who has been thoroughly vetted for their professional skills and expertise (they may not be a BWRT-trained practitioner if they are not listed on the website – if they are, they will have a certificate to say so).

One of the concerns people have about consulting with a professional is the belief that they might get stuck in therapy for years, but nothing could be further from the truth as far as BWRT is concerned. A lot of the time, in

---

1   See https://www.bwrt-professionals.com.

fact, you'll need only two or three visits – and it is not even unusual for relatively simple issues (a phobia or specific anxiety about an exam or a minor medical procedure such as vaccinations) to need only a single session of 40–50 minutes.

Of course, there are some things that might take longer. Deeply entrenched conditions such as alcohol or narcotic dependence, compulsive gambling, OCD, profound depression or unremitting anxiety might need four to six sessions and a follow-up from time to time. But it will still always be a faster therapy than almost any other – and certainly kinder than any other since the BWRT practitioner doesn't need to trawl through childhood looking for any nasties that might be lurking there (which is what happens in many other therapies). Essentially, if you can say how you feel and know how you want to feel instead, BWRT can fix it.

Only the very worst situations, such as those that have made deep and fundamental changes to the way an individual is able to function, might need an extended therapy – but even then, it's still only a few months at most and certainly less than a year. Sufferers of severe PTSD, abuse, sexual assault and similar situations will respond to far fewer sessions than you would ever have thought possible in the past. Whatever it is, there is no longer any need to be scarred for life (unless you want to be, of course).

How they do it

All BWRT practitioners come from the same root: myself, or somebody trained directly by me. As a result, they all adhere to the same strict set of core protocols; whoever you consult with – anywhere in the world – will work in the same manner. So, you can be confident that what you read here is what you get.

As stated right at the very start, the professional model is different from that used in these pages and is considerably more powerful – whatever your presenting difficulty. For a simple direct phobia, such as the fear of spiders or crane flies, the practitioner will begin by explaining the workings of the reptilian complex in more detail than can be covered in this consumer version of the process. That done, they will ask you how you would prefer to feel, instead of how you feel already (they don't use the word lists employed in this version) – then deliver a therapy that will essentially be tailor-made for your personal psychological processes; usually all in one session. In the case of the complex phobia or other multifaceted conditions such as free-floating anxiety, generalised anxiety disorder, poor self-worth, fertility issues (yes, they can work with that too), fear of the future or hypo-chondria, they will need to ask a few more questions to begin with. But these questions are about how you feel, when it started, if you've tried other therapies – all direct questions about the problem itself with abso-lutely no probing into childhood or intimate areas of your private life. In fact, you will never have to tell the practitioner anything that you wish to keep private.

Many practitioners have taken an extra Level 2 training to allow them to work with highly complicated core identity issues including dependencies, destructive habits and other deep-rooted personal issues – even those of a highly intimate nature. For these situations the practitioner needs to know a little more information to provide a successful therapy, so there are a few more questions, but again you will never be requested to disclose personal information that you don't want to share.

Physical illness

The Level 3 practitioners are able to help you cope with chronic and debil-itating illnesses such as chronic fatigue syndrome, fibromyalgia, auto-immune disorders, irritable bowel syndrome, Crohn's disease and more – even including cancer – but they are only able to work with these conditions in conjunction with your GP or medical consultant. The improve-ment that working effectively with your mind can make to the working of your physical body has to be felt to be believed.

Making contact

You can find a full listing of BWRT professional practitioners on the BWRT Professionals website.[2] Most of them work online, or even over the tele-phone – and yes, BWRT is every bit as effective that way as it is in a face-to-face setting. Many offer a free initial consultation to discuss your needs so they can advise on the best treatment for you and arrange for your first (and perhaps only) session.

So here we are at the end of what has, hopefully, been an interesting and rewarding journey – one that's left you feeling better at the end of it than you did at the beginning. Be sure to thoroughly enjoy the New You as you move forward to your Ideal Future!

---

2 See https://www.bwrt-professionals.com.

Bibliography

American Psychological Association (2006). Stress Weakens the Immune System, *Research in Action* [blog] (23 February). Available at https://www.apa.org/research/action/immune.

Ankrom, A. (2021). 8 Deep Breathing Exercises to Reduce Anxiety, *verywellmind* [blog] (20 March). Available at: https://www.verywellmind.com/abdominal-breathing-2584115.

Bühler, K. and Heim, G. (2008). Pierre Janets Konzeption des Unterbewussten [Pierre Janet's Conception of the Subconscious]. *Würzburger medizinhistorische Mitteilungen* 27: 24–62. Available at: https://pubmed.ncbi.nlm.nih.gov/19230366/.

Cassidy, S. (n.d.). "Whether You Think You Can, or You Think You Can't – You're Right." *Advance HE* [blog]. Available at: https://www.heacademy.ac.uk/%E2%80%9Cwhether-you-think-you-can-or-you-think-you-cant-youre-right%E2%80%9D.

Encyclopaedia Britannica, The Editors of (2020). Collective Unconscious, *Encyclopaedia Britannica* (28 February). Available at: https://www.britannica.com/science/collective-unconscious.

Jung, C. G. (2014 [1959]). *Collected Works of C.G. Jung, Volume 9 (Part 1): The Archetypes and the Collective Unconscious*, ed. H. Read, M. Fordham and G. Adler, tr. R. F. C. Hull. Abingdon and New York: Routledge.

Kellermann, N. P. F. (2011). Epigenetic Transmission of Holocaust Trauma: Can Nightmares be Inherited? *Israel Journal of Psychiatry and Related Sciences* 50(1): 33–7.

Kwapis, J. L. and Wood, M. A. (2014). Epigenetic Mechanisms in Fear Conditioning: Implications for Treating Post-Traumatic Stress Disorder. *Trends in Neurosciences* 37(12): 706–720.

Lacal, I. and Ventura, R. (2018). Epigenetic Inheritance: Concepts, Mechanisms and Perspectives. *Frontiers in Molecular Neuroscience* 11: 292. Available at: https://www.frontiersin.org/articles/10.3389/fnmol.2018.00292/full.

Tjornehoj, T. (n.d.). The Relationship Between Anxiety and Depression, *Hartgrove Behavioural Health System* [blog]. Available at: https://www.hartgrovehospital.com/relationship-anxiety-depression/.

Treffert, D. (2015). Genetic Memory: How We Know Things We Never Learned, *Scientific American* [blog] (28 January). Available at: https://blogs.scientificamerican.com/guest-blog/genetic-memory-how-we-know-things-we-never-learned.

Watts, T. (2000). *Warriors, Settlers & Nomads: Discovering Who We Are and What We Can Be*. Carmarthen: Crown House Publishing.

Wolkin, J. (2016). Train Your Brain to Boost Your Immune System, *Mindful* [blog] (23 March). Available at: https://www.mindful.org/train-brain-boost-immune-system/.